**A FEAST OF INFORMATION—**
for people who love to eat but need to know
the sodium count of their meals.

**BARBARA KRAUS 1986 SODIUM
GUIDE TO BRAND NAMES & BASIC FOODS**
lists thousands of basic and ready-to-eat foods
from appetizers to desserts—carry it to the
supermarket, to the restaurant, to the beach, to
the coffee cart, and on trips. Flip through these
fact-filled pages and you'll be able to keep track
of your sodium intake.

# Barbara Kraus
# 1986 Sodium
# Guide to
# Brand Names and
# Basic Foods

D1562553

## SIGNET Books by Barbara Kraus

# Barbara Kraus
# 1986 Sodium
# Guide to
# Brand Names and
# Basic Foods

With *A Note on Sodium* by
Reva T. Frankle, Ed.D., R.D.
Director of Nutrition,
Weight Watchers International, Inc.

A SIGNET BOOK

**NEW AMERICAN LIBRARY**

*Juanita Paet-De Silva and*
*Cheryl Lequeux*

# Foreword

The composition of the foods we eat is not static: it changes from time to time. In the case of *brand-name* products, manufacturers alter their recipes to reflect the availability of ingredients, advances in technology, or improvements in formulae. Each year new products appear on the market and some old ones are discontinued.

On the other hand, information on *basic foods* such as meats, vegetables, and fruits may also change as a result of the development of better analytical methods, different growing conditions, or new marketing practices. These changes, however, are usually relatively small as compared with those in manufactured products.

Some differences may be found between the values in this book and those appearing on the product labels. This is usually due to the fact that the Food and Drug Administration permits manufacturers to round the figures reported on labels. The data in this book are reported as calculated without rounding. If large differences between the two sets of values are noted, they may be due to changes in product formulae, and in those cases the label data should be used.

For all these reasons, a book of nutritive values of foods must be kept up to date by a periodic reviewing and revision of the data presented.

Therefore, this handy sodium counter will provide each year the most current and accurate estimates available.

Good eating in 1986! For 1987, we'll pick up the new products, drop any has-beens, and make whatever other changes are necessary.

*Barbara Kraus*

# A Note on Sodium

by Reva T. Frankle, Ed.D., R.D.
Director of Nutrition,
Weight Watchers International, Inc.

"Excess of salty flavor hardens the pulse."
*The Yellow Emperor's Classic
of Internal Medicine,* circa 1000 B.C

Salt has always been considered the king of seasoning. Historically, it has been associated with social status and wealth. In previous centuries, the most important guests at the table were seated "above the salt," and salt provided the root for the word "salary" (literally, money earned for the purchase of salt).

Today, however, salt's age-old preeminence is being challenged. Research has linked excessive salt consumption with hypertension (high blood pressure), an important risk factor in cardiovascular disease. For this reason, the government's "Dietary Guidelines for Americans," published by the Department of Agriculture in 1980, recommends avoiding too much sodium.

It has been estimated that Americans consume about 10 to 12 grams of salt daily, which amounts to about 2 to 2½ teaspoons. Since salt (sodium chloride) is about 40 percent sodium, this level of salt intake is equal to between 4 and 4½ grams of sodium per day. Where does this salt come from? Of the 10 to 12 grams of salt consumed daily, approximately one-third occurs naturally in foods, one-third comes from salt-containing ingredients added to foods during processing, and one-third represents discretionary salt added by the consumer (from the salt shaker, during cooking, and at the table). Drinking water also contains sodium, the amount varying from locale to locale.

Though there has been much discussion recently about the dangers of salt, let's not lose sight of the fact that sodium, a naturally occurring constituent of all foods, is an essential nutrient. Sodium is a key element in the regulation of body water and plays a vital role in the acid-base balance of the body. In fact sodium, like chloride, is indispensable for many body processes, including the conduction of nerve impulses, heart action, and the function of certain enzyme systems. It's the *excessive* intake of salt that is being questioned.

Today, about 20 percent of the American population has high blood pressure—a primary cause of the 500,000 cases of stroke and the 1.2 million heart attacks that occur each year. High blood pressure is painless, "silent," and therefore often ignored until a complicating event causes it to manifest itself. Yet with proper diet and medical treatment, high blood pressure can be controlled and its complications prevented. For many Americans who suffer this silent disease, a reduced sodium intake is critical. In addition, those people who tend to retain body fluids due to kidney, heart, and liver conditions may want to check with their physicians about a decreased sodium intake. Available evidence indicates that restricting sodium to approximately 3.5 grams of salt per day will effect a slight reduction in blood pressure among moderately hypertensive adults. Several very carefully controlled studies of severely hypertensive adults have shown that sodium must be restricted to 200 milligrams (0.5 grams of salt) per day in order to achieve a significant reduction in blood pressure.

Although efforts to correlate salt intake with the incidence of hypertension have not provided definitive evidence of a causal relationship, nonetheless, evidence seems to indicate there is no risk in lowering present intakes of dietary sodium. The possible link between sodium intake and hypertension has become an issue of increasing concern in the United States. Since hypertension is a potent risk factor for coronary heart disease and stroke, its control is a major health concern. Current treatment of hypertension requires a change in lifestyle—particularly in terms of dietary habits.

A discussion of dietary sodium is complicated. As you will learn as you use this book, some high-sodium foods do not taste salty or are not thought of as salty. For example, an analysis of a serving of fast-food french fries shows 115 milligrams of sodium per serving, whereas a serving of cherry pie has nearly four times this amount, or 450 milligrams.

As a public health nutritionist and a clinical dietitian, may I suggest that in place of salt you sometimes try seasoning foods with some of the following condiments and spices. Onion, garlic, lemon, lime, and vinegar are particularly useful, as are herbs and spices like allspice, aniseed, basil, bay leaf, caraway seed, cardamom, cayenne pepper, celery seed, chili powder, cinnamon, cloves, curry powder, dill seed, fennel seed, garlic, ginger, mace, marjoram, mint, mustard (dry), mustard seed, nutmeg, onion powder, oregano, parsley, pepper, poppy seed, poultry seasoning, rosemary, saffron, sage, sesame seed, tarragon, thyme, turmeric, and vanilla.

Agreed, the sodium intake of Americans is excessive. Since there is no reason to believe that reducing sodium chloride intake would be harmful for healthy persons, and it may even help prevent hypertension in some people, it is time to evaluate our sodium intake. The consumer can meet the challenge of decreasing sodium intake by being aware of the sodium content of foods and using discretion with the salt shaker. There is no specific recommended amount or safety level, but the National Research Council suggests that the estimated safe and adequate daily dietary intake of sodium is about 1100 to 3300 milligrams (1.1 to 3.3 grams). Limiting salt intake to

3 grams per day would allow for some salt to be used in cooking but none at the table.

Industry is responding. Sodium-containing substances such as salt are added to foods for three basic reasons: 1) to provide and enhance flavors in foods, 2) to develop and maintain expected characteristics of foods such as texture and freshness, and 3) as a preservative. Gradual reduction, appropriate for some foods, is taking place. Industry is experimenting with safe new processes for the use of salt, with reduced sodium formulas, and with the use of alternatives to sodium-containing ingredients. Gradual reduction will allow time for industry to determine the microbiologic safety of certain reduced-sodium products.

FDA is working with the processed-food industry on a voluntary basis to lower the sodium content of foods they produce. (Sodium is used almost universally in the preserving and processing of food.) The Department of Health and Human Services is working to give consumers more information about the sodium content of foods they buy, and has said it "would like to see more public awareness in general about sodium and health."

Dietary change is the cornerstone of safe, effective, long-term blood pressure control. How fortunate that we now have *The Barbara Kraus Sodium Guide to Brand Names and Basic Foods,* a comprehensive and easy-to-use book that enables readers to estimate their daily salt intake and to plan a diet that is lower in sodium.

## ABBREVIATIONS AND SYMBOLS

* = prepared as package directs[1]  
< = less than  
& = and  
" = inch  
canned = bottles or jars as well as cans  
dia. = diameter  
fl. = fluid  
liq. = liquid  
lb. = pound  
med. = medium  

oz. = ounce  
pkg. = package  
pt. = pint  
qt. = quart  
sq. = square  
T. = tablespoon  
Tr. = trace  
tsp. = teaspoon  
wt. = weight  

Italics or name in parentheses = registered trademark, ®. All data not identified by company or trademark are based on material obtained from the United States Department of Agriculture or Health, Education and Welfare/Food and Agriculture Organization.

## EQUIVALENTS

| By Weight | By Volume |
|---|---|
| 1 pound = 16 ounces | 1 quart = 4 cups |
| 1 ounce = 28.35 grams | 1 cup = 8 fluid ounces |
| 3.52 ounces = 100 grams | 1 cup = ½ pint |
| 1 gram = 1,000 miligrams | 1 cup = 16 tablespoons |
| | 2 tablespoons = 1 fluid ounce |
| | 1 tablespoon = 3 teaspoons |
| | 1 pound butter = 4 sticks or 2 cups |

[1] If the package directions call for whole or skim milk, the data given here are for whole milk unless otherwise stated.

# A

| Food and Description | Measure or Quantity | Sodium (mgs.) |
|---|---|---|
| **AC'CENT** | ¼ tsp. | 129 |
| **ACEROLA**, fresh, fruit | 4 oz. | 8 |
| **ALBACORE**, raw, meat only | 4 oz. | 45 |
| **ALLSPICE** (French's) | 1 tsp. | 1 |
| **ALMOND:** | | |
| Shelled, raw, natural, with skins | 1 oz. | 1 |
| Roasted, dry (Planters) salted | 1 oz. | 222 |
| Roasted, oil: | | |
| (Fisher) | 1 oz. | 56 |
| (Tom's) | 1 oz. | 180 |
| **ALMOND EXTRACT** | | |
| (Virginia Dare) 34% alcohol | 1 tsp. | 0 |
| *ALPHA-BITS* cereal (Post) | 1 cup (1 oz.) | 219 |
| **ANCHOVY, PICKLED** | | |
| (Granadaisa) | 1 oz. | 1587 |
| **APPLE:** | | |
| Eaten with skin | 2½" dia. | Tr. |
| Eaten without skin | 2½" dia. | Tr. |
| Canned (Comstock): | | |
| Rings, drained | 1 ring | 8 |
| Sliced | ⅙ of 21-oz. can | 30 |
| Dried: | | |
| (Del Monte) | 1 cup | <50 |
| (Sun-Maid) | 2-oz. serving | 40 |
| **APPLE BROWN BETTY** | 1 cup | 350 |
| **APPLE BUTTER** (Smucker's) cider | 1 T. | 1 |
| **APPLE CIDER:** | | |
| Canned (USDA) | ½ cup | 1 |
| *Mix, *Country Time* | 8 fl. oz. | 94 |
| **APPLE-CRANBERRY DRINK** | | |
| (Hi-C): | | |
| Canned | 6 fl. oz. | 23 |
| *Mix | 6 fl. oz. | 11 |
| **APPLE DRINK:** | | |
| Canned: | | |
| *Capri Sun*, natural | 6½ fl.oz. | 2 |

1

| Food and Description | Measure or Quantity | Sodium (mgs.) |
|---|---|---|
| (Hi-C) | 6 fl. oz. | 12 |
| *Mix (Hi-C) | 6 fl. oz. | 20 |
| **APPLE DUMPLINGS,** frozen | | |
| (Pepperidge Farm) | 1 dumpling | 235 |
| **APPLE, ESCALLOPED,** frozen | | |
| (Stouffer's) | 4 oz. | 50 |
| **APPLE-GRAPE JUICE,** canned | | |
| (Red Cheek) | 6 fl. oz. | 2 |
| *APPLE JACKS,* cereal (Kellogg's) | 1 cup (1 oz.) | 125 |
| **APPLE JELLY:** | | |
| Sweetened (Smucker's) | 1 T. | 3 |
| Dietetic: | | |
| (Dia-Mel) | 1 T. | <3 |
| (Diet Delight) | 1 T. | 25 |
| (Louis Sherry) | 1 T. | <3 |
| **APPLE JUICE:** | | |
| Canned: | | |
| (Minute Maid) | 6 fl. oz. | 2 |
| (Mott's) | 6 fl. oz. | <10 |
| (Ocean Spray) | 6 fl. oz. | 14 |
| (Red Cheek) | 6 fl. oz. | 2 |
| Chilled (Minute Maid) | 6 fl. oz. | 2 |
| *Frozen (Minute Maid) | 6 fl. oz. | 2 |
| **APPLE PIE** (See PIE, Apple) | | |
| **APPLE SAUCE:** | | |
| Regular: | | |
| (Comstock) | ½ cup | 90 |
| (Del Monte) | ½ cup | <5 |
| (Mott's) natural style or with | | |
| ground cranberries | ½ cup | <5 |
| (Stokely-Van Camp) | ½ cup | 32 |
| Dietetic: | | |
| (Del Monte) Lite | ½ cup | <10 |
| (Diet Delight) | ½ cup | 5 |
| (Featherweight) water packed | ½ cup | <10 |
| **APPLE STRUDEL,** frozen | | |
| (Pepperidge Farm) | 3 oz. | 215 |
| **APRICOT:** | | |
| Fresh, whole | 1 apricot | Tr. |
| Canned, regular pack: | | |
| (Del Monte) | 1 cup | <10 |
| (Libby's) | 1 cup | 14 |
| (Stokely-Van Camp) | 1 cup | 22 |
| Canned, dietetic: | | |
| (Del Monte) *Lite* | ½ cup | <10 |
| (Diet Delight) | ½ cup | 5 |
| (Featherweight) | ½ cup | <10 |

2

| Food and Description | Measure or Quantity | Sodium (mgs.) |
|---|---|---|
| Dried: | | |
| (Del Monte) | 2 oz. | <10 |
| (Sun-Maid; Sunsweet) | 2 oz. | 3 |
| **APRICOT NECTAR:** | | |
| (Del Monte) | 6 fl. oz. | <10 |
| (Libby's) | 6 fl. oz. | 5 |
| **APRICOT & PINEAPPLE PRESERVE OR JAM:** | | |
| Sweetened (Smucker's) | 1 T. | 3 |
| Dietetic: | | |
| (Diet Delight) | 1 T. | 45 |
| (Featherweight) | 1 T. | 40–50 |
| (Louis Sherry) | 1 T. | <3 |
| **APRICOT SOUR COCKTAIL** | | |
| (National Distillers-*Duet*) 12 ½% alcohol | 2 fl. oz. | Tr. |
| ***ARBY'S:*** | | |
| Arby's Sub, without dressing | 1 sandwich | 1776 |
| Bac'n Cheddar Deluxe | 1 sandwich | 1375 |
| Beef & Cheddar Sandwich | 1 sandwich | 1745 |
| Chicken breast, roasted | 1 piece | 954 |
| Chicken breast, sandwich | 1 sandwich | 1323 |
| Chicken club sandwich | 1 sandwich | 118 |
| Croissant: | | |
| Bacon & egg | 1 sandwich | 550 |
| Butter | 1 sandwich | 225 |
| Ham & swiss | 1 sandwich | 995 |
| Sausage & egg | 1 sandwich | 745 |
| French Dip | 1 sandwich | 1111 |
| Ham 'N Cheese | 1 sandwich | 1745 |
| Potato Cakes | 2 pieces | 476 |
| Potato, stuffed: | | |
| Broccoli & cheese | 1 potato | 480 |
| Deluxe | 1 potato | 480 |
| Taco | 1 potato | 1060 |
| Roast Beef: | | |
| Regular | 1 sandwich | 880 |
| Junior | 1 sandwich | 530 |
| Super | 1 sandwich | 1420 |
| Sauce: | | |
| *Arby's* | 1 oz. | 325 |
| *Horsey* | 1 oz. | 350 |
| Shake: | | |
| Jamocha | 1 shake | 265 |
| Vanilla | 1 shake | 275 |
| Turnover: | | |
| Apple | 1 piece | 240 |

| Food and Description | Measure or Quantity | Sodium (mgs.) |
|---|---|---|
| Cherry | 1 piece | 254 |
| Blueberry | 1 piece | 255 |
| **ARTICHOKE:** | | |
| Boiled | 15-oz. artichoke | 128 |
| Canned (Cara Mia) marinated, drained | 6 oz. jar | 94 |
| Frozen (Birds Eye) deluxe, hearts | ⅓ pkg. | 40 |
| **ASPARAGUS:** | | |
| Boiled | 1 spear (½″ dia. at base) | Tr. |
| Canned, regular pack, spears, solid & liq.: | | |
| (Del Monte) | 4 oz. | 355 |
| (Green Giant) | 4 oz. | 353 |
| (Le Sueur) | 4 oz. | 390 |
| (Stokely-Van Camp) | ½ cup | 448 |
| Canned, dietetic, solids & liq.: | | |
| (Diet Delight) | ½ cup | 5 |
| (S&W) *Nutradiet*, green label | ½ cup | <10 |
| Frozen: | | |
| (Birds Eye): | | |
| Cuts | ⅓ pkg. | Tr. |
| Spears, regular or jumbo deluxe | ⅓ pkg. | 4 |
| (Green Giant) cuts, butter sauce | ½ cup | 725 |
| (McKenzie) Spears | ⅓ pkg. | 4 |
| (Stouffer's) souffle | ⅓ pkg. | 440 |
| ***AUNT JEMIMA SYRUP*** (see SYRUP) | | |
| **AVOCADO,** all varieties | 1 fruit | 11 |
| ***AWAKE*** (Birds Eye) | 6 fl. oz. | 14 |
| **AYDS:** | | |
| Butterscotch, chocolate or chocolate mint | 1 piece | 9 |
| Vanilla | 1 piece | 12 |

# B

| Food and Description | Measure or Quantity | Sodium (mgs.) |
|---|---|---|
| **BACON,** broiled: | | |
| *Black Label* (Hormel) | 1 slice | 149 |
| (Oscar Mayer): | | |
| Regular slice | 6-gr. slice | 114 |
| Thick slice | 1 slice | 209 |
| *Range Brand* (Hormel) | 1 slice | 186 |
| **BACON BITS:** | | |
| *Bac\*Os* (Betty Crocker) | 1 tsp. | 76 |
| (Durkee) imitation | 1 tsp. | 229 |
| (French's) imitation | 1 tsp. | 55 |
| (Hormel) | 1 tsp. | 104 |
| (Oscar Mayer) real | 1 tsp. | 54 |
| **BACON, CANADIAN,** unheated: | | |
| (Eckrich) | 1 oz. | 460 |
| (Hormel) sliced | 1 oz. | 315 |
| (Oscar Mayer) 93% fat free: | | |
| Thin | .7-oz. slice | 295 |
| Thick | 1-oz. slice | 393 |
| **BACON, SIMULATED,** cooked: | | |
| (Oscar Mayer) *Lean 'N Tasty:* | | |
| Beef | 1 slice | 202 |
| Pork | 1 slice | 220 |
| (Swift's) *Sizzlean* | 1 strip | 159 |
| **BAGEL:** | | |
| Egg | 3″-dia. (1.9 oz.) | 245 |
| Water | 3″-dia. (1.9 oz.) | 205 |
| **BAKING POWDER:** | | |
| (Calumet) | 1 tsp. | 396 |
| (Featherweight) low sodium, cereal free | 1 tsp. | 2 |
| **BAMBOO SHOOTS** canned, (La Choy) drained | ¼ cup | <10 |
| **BANANA,** medium (Dole) | 6.2-oz. banana (weighed unpeeled) | 1 |

5

| Food and Description | Measure or Quantity | Sodium (mgs.) |
|---|---|---|
| **BANANA NECTAR** (Libby's) | 6 fl. oz. | 5 |
| **BANANA PIE** (See PIE, Banana) | | |
| **BARBECUE SEASONING** | | |
| (French's) | 1 tsp. | 70 |
| **BARLEY**, pearled (Quaker Scotch) | ¼ cup | 5 |
| **BASIL** (French's) | 1 tsp. | Tr. |
| **BASS**, raw, whole | 1 lb. (weighed whole) | 120 |
| **BAY LEAF** (French's) | 1 tsp. | Tr. |
| **B.B.Q. SAUCE & BEEF**, frozen (Banquet) *Cookin' Bag*, sliced | 4-oz. cooking bag | 929 |
| **BEAN, BAKED:** | | |
| (USDA): | | |
| With pork & molasses sauce | 1 cup | 969 |
| With pork & tomato sauce | 1 cup | 1181 |
| Canned: | | |
| (B&M): | | |
| Pea bean with pork in brown sugar sauce | 8 oz. | 848 |
| Red kidney bean in brown sugar sauce | 8 oz. | 776 |
| (Campbell): | | |
| Home style | 8-oz. can | 1150 |
| With pork & tomato sauce | 8-oz. can | 945 |
| (Friend's) | | |
| Red kidney | 9-oz. can | 1320 |
| Yellow eye | 9-oz. can. | 1470 |
| (Hormel) *Short Orders*, & bacon | 7½ oz. | 813 |
| (Libby's): | | |
| *Deep Brown*, with pork & molasses sauce | ½ of 14-oz. can | 467 |
| *Deep Brown*, vegetarian in tomato sauce | ½ of 14-oz. can | 714 |
| (Van Camp) with pork | 8 oz. | 1005 |
| **BEAN, BARBECUE** (Campbell) | 7⅞-oz. can | 1110 |
| **BEAN, BLACK,** dry | 1 cup | 55 |
| **BEAN, BROWN,** dry | 1 cup | 55 |
| **BEAN & FRANKFURTER,** canned: | | |
| (Campbell) in tomato and molasses sauce | 7⅞-oz. can | 1200 |
| (Hormel) *Short Orders*, 'n weiners | 7½-oz. can | 1342 |
| **BEAN & FRANKFURTER DINNER,** frozen: | | |
| (Banquet) | 10¼-oz. dinner | 1377 |
| (Morton) | 10¾-oz. dinner | 800 |
| (Swanson) | 12½-oz. dinner | 1100 |

| Food and Description | Measure or Quantity | Sodium (mgs.) |
|---|---|---|
| **BEAN, GARBANZO,** canned, dietetic (S&W) *Nutradiet,* low sodium, green label | ½ cup | <10 |
| **BEAN, GREEN:** | | |
| Boiled, 1 ½" to 2" pieces, drained | ½ cup | 4 |
| Canned, regular pack, solids & liq.: | | |
| (Comstock) | ½ cup | 400 |
| (Del Monte) | ½ cup | 355 |
| (Green Giant) french or whole, | ½ cup | 270 |
| (Libby's) french | ½ cup | 335 |
| (Sunshine) | ½ cup | 312 |
| Canned, dietetic, solids & liq.: | | |
| (Del Monte) No Salt Added | ½ cup | <10 |
| (Diet Delight) | ½ cup | <5 |
| (Featherweight) | ½ cup | <10 |
| (Larsen) *Fresh-Lite* | ½ cup | 6 |
| (S&W) *Nutradiet,* cut, green label | ½ cup | <10 |
| Frozen: | | |
| (Birds Eye): | | |
| Cut or french | ⅓ pkg. | 3 |
| French, with almonds | ⅓ pkg. | 336 |
| Whole, deluxe | ⅓ pkg. | 2 |
| (Green Giant): | | |
| With butter sauce | ½ cup | 355 |
| With mushroom in cream sauce | ½ cup | 280 |
| Polybag | ½ cup | 5 |
| (McKenzie) cut or french style | ⅓ pkg. | 3 |
| **BEAN, GREEN & MUSHROOM CASSEROLE** (Stouffer's) | ½ pkg. | 675 |
| **BEAN, GREEN, WITH POTATOES,** canned (Sunshine) solids & liq. | ½ cup | 398 |
| **BEAN, ITALIAN:** | | |
| Canned (Del Monte) solids & liq. | ½ cup | 355 |
| Frozen (Birds Eye) | ⅓ pkg. | 3 |
| **BEAN, KIDNEY** | | |
| Canned, regular pack (Van Camp): | | |
| Light | 8 oz. | 680 |
| New Orleans style | 8 oz. | 793 |
| Red | 8 oz. | 930 |
| Canned, dietetic (S&W) *Nutradiet,* low sodium, solids & liq., green label | ½ cup | <10 |
| **BEAN, LIMA:** | | |
| Boiled, drained | ½ cup | Tr. |
| Canned, regular pack, solids & liq.: | | |
| (Comstock): | | |
| Regular | ½ cup | 400 |

7

| Food and Description | Measure or Quantity | Sodium (mgs.) |
|---|---|---|
| Butter | ½ cup | 500 |
| (Del Monte) | ½ cup | 355 |
| (Libby's) | ½ cup | 247 |
| Canned, dietetic (Featherweight) solids & liq. | ½ cup | 25 |
| Frozen: | | |
| (Birds Eye) tiny, deluxe | ⅓ pkg. | 142 |
| (Green Giant): | | |
| In butter sauce | ½ cup | 445 |
| *Harvest Fresh* | ½ cup | 310 |
| Polybag | ½ cup | 30 |
| (McKenzie): | | |
| Baby lima | ⅓ pkg. | 125 |
| Fordhook | ⅓ pkg. | 71 |
| **BEAN, PINTO** (Del Monte) spicy | ½ cup | 497 |
| **BEAN, REFRIED,** canned: | | |
| (Del Monte) regular | ½ cup | 459 |
| *Old El Paso:* | | |
| With green chili peppers | 4 oz. | 317 |
| With sausage | 4 oz. | 355 |
| **BEAN SALAD,** canned (Green Giant) | 4½-oz. serving | 540 |
| **BEAN SOUP** (See SOUP, Bean) | | |
| **BEAN SPROUT:** | | |
| Mung, raw | ½ lb. | 12 |
| Mung, boiled, drained | ¼ lb. | 5 |
| Canned (La Choy) drained | ⅔ cup | 25 |
| **BEAN, YELLOW OR WAX:** | | |
| Boiled, 1″ pieces, drained | ½ cup | 2 |
| Canned, regular pack, solids & liq.: | | |
| (Comstock) | ½ cup | 370 |
| (Del Monte) | ½ cup | 355 |
| (Libby's) cut | 4 oz. | 336 |
| (Stokely-Van Camp) | ½ cup | 415 |
| Canned, dietetic (Featherweight) cut, solids & liq. | ½ cup | <10 |
| Frozen (McKenzie) cut | ⅓ pkg. | 1 |
| **BEEF,** choice grade, medium done: | | |
| Brisket, braised: | | |
| Lean & fat | 4 oz. | 62 |
| Lean only | 4 oz. | 68 |
| Chuck, pot roast, lean only | 3 oz. | 51 |
| Filet Mignon (See Steak, sirloin, lean) | | |
| Flank, braised, 100% lean | 3 oz. | 51 |
| Ground: | | |
| Regular, raw | ½ cup | 73 |

| Food and Description | Measure or Quantity | Sodium (mgs.) |
|---|---|---|
| Regular, broiled | 3 oz. | 39 |
| Lean, broiled | 3 oz. | 40 |
| Rib Roasted, lean & fat | 3 oz. | 51 |
| Round: | | |
| Broiled, lean & fat | 3 oz. | 51 |
| Lean only | 3 oz. | 51 |
| Steak, club, broiled: | | |
| One 8-oz. steak (weighed without bone before cooking) will give you: | | |
| Lean & fat | 5.9 oz. | 68 |
| Lean only | 3.4 oz. | 68 |
| Steak, porterhouse, broiled: | | |
| One 16-oz. steak (weighed with bone before cooking) will give you: | | |
| Lean & fat | 4 oz. | 68 |
| Lean only | 5.9 oz. | 72 |
| **BEEFAMATO COCKTAIL** (Mott's) | 6 fl. oz. | 240 |
| **BEEF BOUILLON:** | | |
| (Herb-Ox): | | |
| Cube | 1 cube | 500 |
| Packet | 1 packet | 1040 |
| *MBT* | 1 packet | 755 |
| Low sodium (Featherweight) | 1 tsp. | 10 |
| **BEEF, CHIPPED, CREAMED,** | | |
| Frozen: | | |
| (Banquet) *Cookin' Bag* | 4-oz. pkg. | 1082 |
| (Morton) | 5-oz. pkg. | 1370 |
| (Stouffer's) | 5½ serving | 900 |
| (Swanson) | 10½-oz. entree | 1545 |
| **BEEF DINNER or ENTREE,** frozen: | | |
| (Banquet): | | |
| American Favorite, chopped | 11-oz. dinner | 1199 |
| Extra Helping, sliced | 16-oz. dinner | 1792 |
| (Green Giant) teriyaki | 10-oz. entree | 780 |
| (Le Menu): | | |
| Chopped sirloin | 11½-oz. dinner | 825 |
| Yankee pot roast | 11-oz. dinner | 830 |
| (Morton): | | |
| Regular | 10-oz. dinner | 840 |
| *Country Table,* sliced | 14-oz. dinner | 1220 |
| *Steak House,* sirloin strip | 9½-oz. dinner | 390 |
| (Stouffer's) *Lean Cuisine,* oriental | 8⅝-oz. pkg. | 1150 |
| (Swanson): | | |
| Regular, chopped sirloin | 11½-oz. dinner | 915 |

| Food and Description | Measure or Quantity | Sodium (mgs.) |
|---|---|---|
| *Hungry Man:* | | |
| Chopped | 17¼-oz. dinner | 2030 |
| Sliced | 12¼-oz. entree | 1045 |
| (Weight Watchers): | | |
| Beefsteak, 2-compartment meal | 9¾-oz. pkg. | 1115 |
| Oriental | 10-oz. dinner | 1134 |
| Sirloin in mushroom sauce, 3-compartment meal | 13-oz. pkg. | 1426 |
| **BEEF, DRIED,** packaged: | | |
| (Hormel) sliced | 1 oz. | 822 |
| (Swift) | ¾ oz. | 505 |
| **BEEF, PACKAGED** (Hormel) | 1 oz. | 382 |
| **BEEF, GROUND, SEASONING MIX:** | | |
| *(Durkee): | | |
| Regular | 1 cup | 799 |
| With onion | 1 cup | 1099 |
| (French's) with onion | 1⅛-oz. pkg. | 1760 |
| **BEEF HASH, ROAST:** | | |
| Canned, *Mary Kitchen* (Hormel): | | |
| Regular | 7½-oz. serving | 1142 |
| *Short Orders* | 7½-oz. can | 1156 |
| Frozen (Stouffer's) | ½ of 11½-oz. can | 760 |
| **BEEF PEPPER ORIENTAL** | | |
| Frozen (La Choy) | 12-oz. entree | 1690 |
| **BEEF PIE,** frozen: | | |
| (Banquet): | | |
| Regular | 8-oz. pie | 964 |
| Supreme | 8-oz. pie | 1245 |
| (Morton) | 8-oz. pie. | 1040 |
| (Swanson): | | |
| Regular | 8-oz. pie | 810 |
| *Hungry Man*, regular | 16-oz. pie | 1565 |
| **BEEF ROLL** (Hormel) Lumberjack | 1 oz. | 304 |
| **BEEF, SHORT RIBS,** frozen (Stouffer's) boneless, with vegetable gravy | ½ of 11½-oz. pkg. | 560 |
| **BEEF SOUP** (See SOUP, Beef) | | |
| **BEEF SPREAD, ROAST,** canned (Underwood) | ½ of 4¾-oz. can | 515 |
| **BEEF STEW:** | | |
| Home recipe, made with lean beef chuck | 1 cup | 91 |
| Canned, regular pack: | | |
| *Dinty Moore* (Hormel): | | |
| Regular | 8-oz. serving | 980 |
| *Short Orders* | 7½-oz. can | 939 |
| (Swanson) | 7⅝-oz. serving | 890 |

| Food and Description | Measure or Quantity | Sodium (mgs.) |
|---|---|---|
| Canned, dietetic: | | |
| (Dia-Mel) | 8-oz. serving | 70 |
| (Featherweight) | 7½-oz. serving | 96 |
| Frozen: | | |
| (Banquet) *Buffet Supper* | 2-lb. pkg. | 3908 |
| (Green Giant) *Boil'N Bag:* | 9-oz. entree | 275 |
| (Morton) *Family Meal* | 2-lb. pkg. | 1980 |
| (Stouffer's) | 10-oz. serving | 1675 |
| **BEEF STEW SEASONING MIX:** | | |
| *(Durkee) | 1 cup | 975 |
| (French's) | 1 pkg. | 4590 |
| **BEEF STOCK BASE** (French's) | 1 tsp. | 500 |
| **BEEF STROGANOFF,** frozen | | |
| (Stouffer's) with parsley noodles | 9¾ oz. | 1300 |
| ***BEEF STROGANOFF SEASONING** | | |
| **MIX** (Durkee) | 1 cup | 870 |
| **BEER & ALE:** | | |
| Regular: | | |
| *Black Horse Ale* | 8 fl. oz. | 33 |
| *Budweiser* | 8 fl. oz. | 12 |
| *Busch Bavarian* | 8 fl. oz. | 5-15 |
| *Michelob* | 8 fl. oz. | 5-15 |
| Light or low carbohydrate: | | |
| *Budweiser Light* | 8 fl. oz. | 5-15 |
| *Gablinger's* | 8 fl. oz. | 14 |
| *Michelob Light* | 8 fl. oz. | 5-15 |
| *Natural Light* | 8 fl. oz. | 5-15 |
| **BEER, NEAR:** | | |
| *Kingsbury* (Heileman) | 8 fl. oz. | 19 |
| (Metbrew) | 8 fl. oz. | 18 |
| **BEET:** | | |
| Boiled, without salt, sliced | ½ cup | 44 |
| Boiled, without salt, whole | 2"-dia. butt | 21 |
| Canned, regular pack solids & liq.: | | |
| (Blue Boy) | ½ cup | 350 |
| (Del Monte): | | |
| Pickled | 4 oz. | 375 |
| Sliced | ½ cup | 290 |
| (Greenwood): | | |
| Harvard | ½ cup | 350 |
| Pickled | ½ cup | 250 |
| (Libby's) Harvard | ½ cup | 161 |
| (Stokely-Van Camp) pickled | ½ cup | 290 |
| Canned, dietetic, solids & liq.: | | |
| (Comstock) | ½ cup | 100 |
| (Del Monte) No Salt Added | ½ cup | 100 |
| (Featherweight) sliced | ½ cup | 55 |

| Food and Description | Measure or Quantity | Sodium (mgs.) |
|---|---|---|
| (Larsen) *Fresh-Lite* | ½ cup | 49 |
| (S&W) *Nutradiet,* sliced, green label | ½ cup | 40 |
| **BIG H,** burger sauce (Hellman's) | 1 T. | 143 |
| **BIG MAC** (*See McDONALD'S*) | | |
| **BIG WHEEL** (Hostess) | 1 piece | 130 |
| **BITTERS** (Angostura) | 1 tsp. | Tr |
| **BLACKBERRY JELLY:** | | |
| Sweetened (Smucker's) | 1 T. | 4 |
| Dietetic: | | |
| (Diet Delight) | 1 T. | 45 |
| (Featherweight) | 1 T. | 40-50 |
| **BLACKBERRY PRESERVE OR JAM:** | | |
| Sweetened (Smucker's) | 1 T. | 2 |
| Dietetic: | | |
| (Dia-Mel) | 1 T. | <3 |
| (Featherweight) | 1 T. | 40-50 |
| (Louis Sherry) | 1 T. | <3 |
| **BLACK-EYED PEAS:** | | |
| Canned, with pork, solids & liq., (Sunshine) | ½ cup | 464 |
| Frozen: | | |
| (Birds Eye) | ⅓ pkg. | 6 |
| (McKenzie) | ⅓ pkg. | 6 |
| **BLINTZE,** frozen (King Kold) cheese | 2½-oz. piece | 250 |
| **BLOODY MARY MIX,** dry (Bar-Tender's) | 1 serving | 510 |
| **BLUEBERRY,** fresh, whole | ½ lb. | 2 |
| **BLUEBERRY PIE** (See PIE, Blueberry) | | |
| **BLUEBERRY PRESERVE OR JAM:** | | |
| Sweetened (Smucker's) | 1 T. | 6 |
| Dietetic (Dia-Mel) | 1 T. | <3 |
| **BLUEFISH,** broiled | 3½" × 3" × ½" piece | 130 |
| **BODY BUDDIES,** cereal (General Mills): | | |
| Brown sugar & honey | 1 cup | 290 |
| Natural fruit flavor | ¾ cup | 285 |
| **BOLOGNA:** | | |
| (Eckrich): | | |
| Beef | 1-oz. | 280 |
| Beef, thick slice | 1.8-oz. | 510 |
| Garlic | 1-oz. slice | 290 |
| German brand | 1-oz. slice | 350 |
| Meat, thick sliced | 1.7-oz. slice | 490 |

| Food and Description | Measure or Quantity | Sodium (mgs.) |
|---|---|---|
| (Hormel): | | |
| Beef | 1-oz. slice | 296 |
| Meat | 1-oz. slice | 300 |
| (Oscar Mayer): | | |
| Beef | .8-oz. slice | 239 |
| Beef | 1-oz. slice | 295 |
| Beef | 1.3-oz. slice | 394 |
| Meat | .8-oz. slice | 241 |
| Meat | 1-oz. slice | 298 |
| (Swift) | 1-oz. slice | 307 |
| **BOLOGNA & CHEESE:** | | |
| (Eckrich) | .7-oz. slice | 290 |
| (Oscar Mayer) | .8-oz. slice | 244 |
| ***BOO\*BERRY*,** cereal (General Mills) | 1 cup | 210 |
| **BORSCHT,** canned: | | |
| Regular (Mother's) old fashioned | 8-oz. serving | 907 |
| Dietetic or low calorie (Mother's): | | |
| Artificially sweetened | 8-oz. serving | 943 |
| Unsalted | 8-oz. serving | 51 |
| ***BOSCO*** (see SYRUP) | | |
| **BOYSENBERRY JELLY,** sweetened | | |
| (Smucker's) | 1 T. | 3 |
| **BRAN:** | | |
| Crude | 1 oz. | 3 |
| Miller's (Elam's) | 1 oz. | 6 |
| **BRAN BREAKFAST CEREAL:** | | |
| (Kellogg's): | | |
| *All Bran* | ⅓ cup | 270 |
| *Bran Buds* | ⅓ cup | 150 |
| *Cracklin' Oat Bran* | ½ cup | 190 |
| 40% bran flakes | ¾ cup | 220 |
| Raisin | ¾ cup | 210 |
| (Loma Linda) | 1 oz. | 115 |
| (Post) 40% bran flakes | ⅔ cup | 260 |
| (Quaker) *Corn Bran* | ⅔ cup | 245 |
| (Ralston-Purina): | | |
| *Bran Chex* | ⅔ cup | 267 |
| 40% bran | ¾ cup | 294 |
| Raisin | ¾ cup | 286 |
| **BRAUNSCHWEIGER:** | | |
| (Eckrich) chub | 1 oz. | 400 |
| (Hormel) | 1 oz. | 322 |
| (Oscar Mayer) chub | 1 oz. | 335 |
| (Swift) 8-oz. chub | 1 oz. | 282 |
| **BRAZIL NUT:** | | |
| Shelled | 4 nuts | Tr. |
| Roasted (Fisher) | 1 oz. | 57 |

| Food and Description | Measure or Quantity | Sodium (mgs.) |
|---|---|---|
| **BREAD:** | | |
| Apple (Pepperidge Farm) with cinnamon | .9-oz. slice | 105 |
| Boston Brown | 3" × ¾" slice | 120 |
| Bran'nola (Arnold) | 1.2-oz. slice | 178 |
| Cinnamon (Pepperidge Farm) | .9-oz. slice | 98 |
| Corn & Molasses (Pepperidge Farm) | .9-oz. slice | 130 |
| Cracked wheat: | | |
| (Pepperidge Farm) | .9-oz. slice | 130 |
| (Wonder) | 1-oz. slice | 181 |
| Crispbrad, *Wasa:* | | |
| Mora | 3.2-oz. slice | 514 |
| Rye, golden | .4-oz slice | 43 |
| Rye, lite | .3-oz. slice | 20 |
| Sesame | .5-oz. slice | 35 |
| Sport | .4-oz. slice | 66 |
| Date walnut (Pepperidge Farm) | .9-oz. slice | 108 |
| Flatbread, *Ideal:* | | |
| Bran | .2-oz. slice | 47 |
| Extra thin | .1-oz slice | 25 |
| Whole grain | .2-oz. slice | 47 |
| French: | | |
| (Pepperidge Farm) | 2-oz. slice | 430 |
| (Wonder) | 1-oz. slice | 180 |
| *Hillbilly* | 1-oz. slice | 140 |
| *Hollywood*, dark | 1-oz. slice | 160 |
| Honey bran (Pepperidge Farm) | 1 slice | 207 |
| Honey wheat berry: | | |
| (Arnold) | 1.2-oz. slice | 205 |
| (Pepperidge Farm) | 1.2-oz. slice | 105 |
| Italian (Pepperidge Farm) | 2-oz. slice | 320 |
| Multi-grain (Pepperidge Farm) | .5-oz. slice | 75 |
| Oatmeal (Pepperidge Farm) | .9-oz. slice | 185 |
| Onion (Pepperidge Farm) party | .2-oz. slice | 25 |
| Orange & Raisin (Pepperidge Farm) | .9-oz. slice | 88 |
| Protein (Thomas') | .7-oz. slice | 94 |
| Pumpernickel: | | |
| (Arnold) | 1.1-oz. slice | 230 |
| (Levy's) | 1.1-oz. slice | 192 |
| (Pepperidge Farm): | | |
| Regular | 1.1-oz. slice | 305 |
| Party | .2-oz. slice | 55 |
| Raisin: | | |
| (Arnold) tea | .9-oz. slice | 112 |
| (Pepperidge Farm) | 1 slice | 107 |
| (Thomas') cinnamon | .8-oz. slice | 92 |
| *Roman Meal* | 1-oz. slice | 140 |

| Food and Description | Measure or Quantity | Sodium (mgs.) |
|---|---|---|
| Rye: | | |
| (Arnold) Jewish, with seeds | 1.1-oz. slice | 212 |
| (Levy's) real | 1-oz. slice | 185 |
| (Pepperidge Farm): | | |
| Family | 1.1-oz. slice | 242 |
| Jewish | 1.1-oz. slice | 278 |
| Party | .2-oz. slice | 104 |
| (Wonder) | 1-oz. slice | 180 |
| *Sahara* (Thomas'): | | |
| Wheat | 1-oz. piece | 188 |
| White | 1-oz. piece | 145 |
| Sourdough, *Di Carlo* | 1-oz. slice | 180 |
| Sprouted wheat (Pepperidge Farm) | .9-oz. slice | 113 |
| Vienna (Pepperidge Farm) | .9-oz. slice | 175 |
| Wheat (see also Cracked Wheat): | | |
| (Arnold) *Bran'nola* | 1.3-oz. slice | 222 |
| *Fresh Horizons* | 1-oz. slice | 140 |
| *Fresh & Natural* | 1-oz. slice | 140 |
| *Home Pride* | 1-oz. slice | 140 |
| (Pepperidge Farm) sandwich | .8-oz. slice | 115 |
| (Wonder) family | 1-oz. slice | 140 |
| Wheatberry, *Home Pride*, honey | 1-oz. slice | 160 |
| Wheat Germ (Pepperidge Farm) | .9-oz. slice | 145 |
| White: | | |
| (Arnold): | | |
| *Brick Oven* | .8-oz. slice | 102 |
| Country | 1.2-oz. slice | 245 |
| *Measure Up* | .5-oz. slice | 68 |
| *Fresh Horizons* | 1-oz. slice | 140 |
| *Home Pride* | 1-oz. slice | 160 |
| (Pepperidge Farm): | | |
| Large loaf | .9-oz. slice | 175 |
| Sandwich | .8-oz. slice | 140 |
| Sliced, 1-lb. loaf | .9-oz. slice | 168 |
| Toasting | 1.2-oz. slice | 240 |
| (Wonder) regular | 1-oz. slice | 140 |
| Whole wheat: | | |
| (Arnold) *Brick Oven* | .8-oz. slice | 80 |
| (Pepperidge Farm) thin slice | 1 slice | 145 |
| (Thomas') 100% | .8-oz. slice | 118 |
| (Wonder) 100% | 1-oz. slice | 160 |
| **BREAD, CANNED,** brown, plain or raisin (B&M) | ½" slice | 220 |
| **BREAD CRUMBS:** | | |
| (Contadina) seasoned | ½ cup (2.1 oz.) | 1580 |
| (Pepperidge Farm): | | |
| Regular | 1-oz. | 255 |
| Herb Seasoned | 1-oz. | 260 |

| Food and Description | Measure or Quantity | Sodium (mgs.) |
|---|---|---|
| **\*BREAD DOUGH, FROZEN:** | | |
| (Pepperidge Farm): | | |
| Country rye | 1/10 loaf | 185 |
| Stone ground wheat | 1/10 loaf | 127 |
| White | 1/10 loaf | 165 |
| (Rich's): | | |
| French | 1/20 loaf | 138 |
| Italian | 1/20 loaf | 300 |
| Raisin | 1/20 loaf | 107 |
| Wheat | .5-oz. slice | 375 |
| White | .8-oz. slice | 96 |
| **BREAD DOUGH, REFRIGERATED** | | |
| (Pillsbury) *Poppin Fresh* | 1/16 of loaf | 195 |
| **\*BREAD MIX** (Pillsbury): | | |
| Applesauce spice, blueberry nut or cranberry | 1/12 of loaf | 155 |
| Carrot nut | 1/12 of loaf | 170 |
| Cherry nut | 1/12 of loaf | 150 |
| Nut | 1/12 of loaf | 180 |
| **BREAD PUDDING,** with raisins | ½ cup | 278 |
| **BREAD STICK DOUGH,** | | |
| refrigerated (Pillsbury) *Pipin' Hot* | 1 piece | 240 |
| **\*BREAKFAST DRINK** (Pillsbury) | 1 pouch | 180 |
| **BREAKFAST SQUARES** | | |
| (General Mills) all flavors | 1 bar | 255 |
| **BROCCOLI:** | | |
| Raw, large leaves removed | 1 lb. (weighed trimmed) | 53 |
| Boiled, whole stalk | 1 stalk | 19 |
| Boiled, ½" pieces | ½ cup | 20 |
| Frozen: | | |
| (Birds Eye): | | |
| In cheese sauce | 1/3 pkg. | 337 |
| Chopped | 1/3 pkg. | 18 |
| Spears in butter sauce | 1/3 pkg. | 379 |
| (Green Giant): | | |
| Cuts, polybag | ½ cup | 10 |
| *Harvest Fresh* | 4 oz. | 160 |
| Spears in butter sauce | 3 1/3 oz. | 325 |
| (McKenzie) chopped or spears | 1/3 pkg. | 18 |
| (Stouffer's) in cheese sauce | 4½-oz. serving | 970 |
| **BROTH & SEASONING:** | | |
| (George Washington) golden | 1 packet | 1093 |
| *Maggi* | 1 T. | 923 |
| **BRUSSELS SPROUT:** | | |
| Boiled | 3-4 sprouts | 8 |

| Food and Description | Measure or Quantity | Sodium (mgs.) |
|---|---|---|
| Frozen: | | |
| (Birds Eye): | | |
| Regular | ⅓ pkg. | 15 |
| Baby, with cheese sauce | ⅓ pkg. | 291 |
| Baby, deluxe | ⅓ pkg. | 9 |
| (Green Giant): | | |
| In butter sauce | ½ cup. | 275 |
| Halves in cheese sauce | ½ cup | 475 |
| Polybag | ½ cup | 15 |
| **BUC*WHEATS,** cereal | | |
| (General Mills) | 1 oz. (¾ cup) | 235 |
| **BULGUR,** canned, seasoned | 4 oz. | 522 |
| **BURGER KING:** | | |
| Apple pie | 3-oz. pie | 385 |
| Cheeseburger | 1 burger | 705 |
| Cheeseburger, double bacon | 1 burger | 985 |
| Cheeseburger, double meat | 1 burger | 865 |
| Chicken sandwich | 1 sandwich | 775 |
| French fries | 1 regular order | 230 |
| Hamburger | 1 burger | 560 |
| Hamburger, double | 1 burger | 585 |
| Ham & cheese sandwich | 1 sandwich | 1550 |
| Onion rings | 1 regular order | 450 |
| *Pepsi,* diet | 1 medium-sized drink | 52 |
| Shake, chocolate | 1 shake | 320 |
| Veal parmigiana | 1 sandwich | 805 |
| *Whaler:* | | |
| Regular | 1 sandwich | 745 |
| With cheese | 1 sandwich | 885 |
| *Whopper:* | | |
| Regular | 1 burger | 975 |
| Regular, with cheese | 1 burger | 1260 |
| Double beef | 1 burger | 1015 |
| Double beef, with cheese | 1 burger | 1295 |
| Junior | 1 burger | 545 |
| Junior with cheese | 1 burger | 685 |
| **BURGUNDY WINE:** | | |
| (Gold Seal) | 3 fl. oz. | 3 |
| (Great Western) | 3 fl. oz. | 36 |
| **BURGUNDY WINE, SPARKLING:** | | |
| (B&G) | 3 fl. oz. | 2 |
| (Gold Seal) | 3 fl. oz. | 3 |
| **BURRITO:** | | |
| *Canned (Del Monte) | 1 burrito | 616 |
| Frozen: | | |
| (Hormel): | | |
| Beef | 1 burrito | 780 |

| Food and Description | Measure or Quantity | Sodium (mgs.) |
|---|---|---|
| Cheese | 1 burrito | 792 |
| Chicken & rice | 1 burrito | 594 |
| Hot chili | 1 burrito | 619 |
| (Van de Kamp's) & guacamole sauce | 6-oz. serving | 652 |
| **BURRITO FILLING MIX,** canned | | |
| (Del Monte) | ½ cup | 900 |
| **BUTTER:** | | |
| Regular: | | |
| (Breakstone): | | |
| Salted | 1 T. (.5 oz.) | 95 |
| Unsalted | 1 T. | Tr. |
| (Sealtest) | 1 T. | 117 |
| Whipped (Breakstone): | | |
| Salted | 1 T. (.3 oz.) | 64 |
| Unsalted | 1 T. | Tr. |
| **BUTTERSCOTCH MORSELS** | | |
| (Nestlé) | 1 oz. | 15 |

# C

| Food and Description | Measure or Quantity | Sodium (mgs.) |
|---|---|---|
| **CABBAGE:** | | |
| Boiled, without salt | ½ cup | 10 |
| Canned, solids & liq. (Comstock) red | ½ cup | 480 |
| Frozen (Green Giant) stuffed, in tomato sauce | ½ of pkg. | 800 |
| **CAKE:** | | |
| Regular, non-frozen: | | |
| Plain, home recipe, with butter, with boiled white icing | ⅑ of 9″ square | 299 |
| Angel food, home recipe | 1/12 of 8″ cake | 113 |
| Caramel, home recipe, with caramel icing | ⅑ of 9″ square | 214 |
| Carrot (Hostess) | 3-oz. serving | 179 |
| Chocolate, home recipe, with chocolate icing, 2-layer | 1/16 of 10″ cake | 282 |
| Crumb (Hostess) | 1¼-oz. cake | 95 |
| Fruit: | | |
| Home recipe, dark | 1/30 of 8″ loaf | 24 |
| Home recipe, made with butter | 1/30 of 8″ loaf | 29 |
| (Holland Honey Cake) unsalted | 1/14 of cake | 2 |
| Pound, home recipe, traditional, made with butter | 3½″ × 3½″ slice | 53 |
| Raisin Date Loaf (Holland Honey Cake) low sodium | 1/14 of 13-oz. cake | 2 |
| Sponge, home recipe | 1/12 of 10″ cake | 110 |
| White, home recipe, made with butter, without icing, 2-layer | ⅑ of 9″ wide, 3″ high cake | 280 |
| Yellow, home recipe, made with butter, without icing, 2-layer | 1/19 of cake | 225 |
| Frozen: | | |
| Apple Walnut: | | |
| (Pepperidge Farm) with cream cheese icing | ⅛ of 11¾-oz. cake | 140 |

| Food and Description | Measure or Quantity | Sodium (mgs.) |
|---|---|---|
| (Sara Lee) | ⅛ of 12½-oz. cake | 140 |
| Banana (Sara Lee) | ⅛ of 13¾-oz. cake | 154 |
| Boston cream (Pepperidge Farm) | ¼ of 11¾-oz. cake | 190 |
| Carrot (Pepperidge Farm) with cream cheese icing | ⅛ of 11¾-oz. cake | 145 |
| Carrot (Weight Watchers) | 2⅝-oz. serving | 261 |
| Cheesecake: | | |
| (Morton) *Great Little Desserts:* | | |
|   Cherry or cream cheese | 6-oz. cake | 350 |
|   Pineapple | 6-oz. cake | 355 |
|   Strawberry | 6-oz. cake | 350 |
| (Rich's) Viennese | 1/14 of 42-oz. cake | 297 |
| (Sara Lee): | | |
|   Blueberry, *For 2* | ½ of 11.3-oz. cake | 326 |
|   Cream cheese: | | |
|     Regular | ⅓ of 10-oz. cake | 206 |
|     Blueberry | ⅙ of 19-oz. cake | 175 |
|     Cherry | ⅙ of 19-oz. cake | 185 |
|     Strawberry | ⅙ of 19-oz. cake | 170 |
|     Strawberry, French | ⅛ of 26-oz. cake | 128 |
|     Strawberry, *For 2* | ½ of 11.3-oz. cake | 268 |
| (Weight Watchers) regular | 4-oz. serving | 287 |
| Chocolate: | | |
| (Pepperidge Farm): | | |
|   Layer, fudge | 1/10 of 17-oz. cake | 140 |
|   *Rich 'N Moist* with chocolate icing | ⅛ of 14¼-oz. cake | 160 |
|   Supreme | ¼ of 11½-oz. cake | 140 |
| (Sara Lee): | | |
|   Regular | ⅛ of 13¼-oz. cake | 168 |
|   Bavarian | ⅛ of 22½-oz. cake | 78 |
|   German | ⅛ of 12¼-oz. cake | 134 |
|   Layer'n cream | ⅛ of 18-oz. cake | 136 |
| Coffee (Sara Lee): | | |
|   Almond | ⅛ of 11¾-oz. cake | 158 |
|   Almond ring | ⅛ of 9½-oz. cake | 124 |
|   Apple | ⅛ of 15-oz. cake | 208 |
|   Apple, *For 2* | ½ of 9-oz. cake | 502 |
|   Butter, *For 2* | ½ of 6½-oz. cake | 391 |
|   Maple crunch ring | ⅛ of 9¾-oz. cake | 131 |
|   Pecan | ⅛ of 11¼-oz. cake | 159 |
|   Streusel, butter | ⅛ of 11½-oz. cake | 178 |
|   Streusel, cinnamon | ⅛ of 10.9-oz. cake | 156 |
| Crumb (See ROLL OR BUN, Crumb) | | |
| Devil's food (Pepperidge Farm) layer | 1/10 of 17-oz. cake | 135 |

| Food and Description | Measure or Quantity | Sodium (mgs.) |
|---|---|---|
| Golden (Pepperidge Farm) layer | ⅒ of 17-oz. cake | 115 |
| Lemon coconut (Pepperidge Farm) | ¼ of 12¼-oz. cake | 220 |
| Orange (Sara Lee) | ⅛ of 13¾-oz. cake | 170 |
| Pineapple cream (Pepperidge Farm) Supreme | 1/12 of 24-oz. cake | 145 |
| Pound (Sara Lee): | | |
|   Regular | ⅒ of 10¾-oz. cake | 104 |
|   Banana nut | ⅒ of 11-oz. cake | 104 |
|   Chocolate | ⅒ of 10¾-oz. cake | 134 |
|   Family size | 1/15 of 16½-oz. cake | 106 |
|   Homestyle | ⅒ of 9½-oz. cake | 97 |
| Spice (Weight Watchers) | 2⅝-oz. serving | 251 |
| Strawberry cream (Pepperidge Farm) Supreme | 1/12 of 24-oz. cake | 145 |
| Strawberries'n cream, layer (Sara Lee) | ⅛ of 20½-oz. cake | 150 |
| Torte (Sara Lee): | | |
|   Apples'n cream | ⅛ of 21-oz. cake | 146 |
|   Fudge & nut | ⅛ of 15¾-oz. cake | 144 |
|   Vanilla (Pepperidge Farm) layer | ⅒ of 17-oz. cake | 120 |
|   Walnut, layer (Sara Lee) | ⅛ of 18-oz. cake | 102 |
| Yellow (Pepperidge Farm) *Rich n' Moist* | ⅛ of 12½-oz. cake | 120 |
| **CAKE OR COOKIE ICING** | | |
| (Pillsbury) all flavors | 1 T. | 5 |
| **CAKE ICING:** | | |
| Butter pecan (Betty Crocker) *Creamy Deluxe* | 1/12 of can | 85 |
| Caramel, home recipe | 4 oz. | 94 |
| Cherry (Betty Crocker) *Creamy Deluxe* | 1/12 can | 95 |
| Chocolate: | | |
|   (Betty Crocker) *Creamy Deluxe*: | | |
|     Regular | 1/12 can | 95 |
|     Chip | 1/12 can | 85 |
|     Fudge dark | 1/12 can | 125 |
|     Milk | 1/12 can | 95 |
|     Sour cream | 1/12 can | 110 |
|   (Duncan Hines) regular | 1/12 can | 84 |
|   (Pillsbury) *Frosting Supreme*: | | |
|     Fudge | 1/12 can | 80 |
|     Milk | 1/12 can | 60 |
|     Mint | 1/12 can | 80 |
| Coconut almond (Pillsbury) *Frosting Supreme* | 1/12 can | 60 |
| Cream cheese: | | |
|   (Betty Crocker) *Creamy Deluxe* | 1/12 can | 100 |

| Food and Description | Measure or Quantity | Sodium (mgs.) |
|---|---|---|
| (Pillsbury) *Frosting Supreme* | ⅟₁₂ can | 115 |
| Double dutch (Pillsbury) | | |
| *Frosting Supreme* | ⅟₁₂ can | 45 |
| Orange (Betty Crocker) | | |
| *Creamy Deluxe* | ⅟₁₂ can | 95 |
| Strawberry (Pillsbury) | | |
| *Frosting Supreme* | ⅟₁₂ can | 75 |
| Vanilla: | | |
| (Betty Crocker) *Creamy Deluxe* | ⅟₁₂ can | 95 |
| (Duncan Hines) | ⅟₁₂ can | 86 |
| (Pillsbury) *Frosting Supreme* | ⅟₁₂ can | 80 |
| White: | | |
| Home recipe, boiled | 4 oz. | 162 |
| Home recipe, uncooked | 4 oz. | 56 |
| (Betty Crocker) *Creamy Deluxe* | ⅟₁₂ can | 95 |
| **\*CAKE ICING MIX:** | | |
| Regular: | | |
| Banana (Betty Crocker) *Chiquita*, creamy | ⅟₁₂ pkg. | 100 |
| *Butter Brickle* (Betty Crocker) creamy | ⅟₁₂ pkg. | 115 |
| Butter pecan (Betty Crocker) creamy | ⅟₁₂ pkg. | 100 |
| Caramel (Pillsbury) *Rich'n Easy* | ⅟₁₂ pkg. | 35 |
| Cherry (Betty Crocker) creamy | ⅟₁₂ pkg. | 100 |
| Chocolate: | | |
| Home recipe, fudge | 1 cup | 354 |
| (Betty Crocker) creamy: | | |
| Fluffy, almond fudge | ⅟₁₂ pkg. | 75 |
| Fudge, creamy | ⅟₁₂ pkg. | 75 |
| Fudge, creamy, dark | ⅟₁₂ pkg. | 90 |
| (Pillsbury) *Rich'n Easy*, fudge | ⅟₁₂ pkg. | 70 |
| Coconut almond (Pillsbury) | ⅟₁₂ pkg. | 90 |
| Coconut pecan: | | |
| (Betty Crocker) creamy | ⅟₁₂ pkg. | 100 |
| (Pillsbury) | ⅟₁₂ pkg. | 105 |
| Cream cheese & nut (Betty Crocker) creamy | ⅟₁₂ pkg. | 100 |
| Lemon: | | |
| (Betty Crocker) *Sunkist*, creamy | ⅟₁₂ pkg. | 100 |
| (Pillsbury) *Rich'n Easy* | ⅟₁₂ pkg. | 15 |
| Strawberry (Pillsbury) *Rich'n Easy* | ⅟₁₂ pkg. | 55 |
| Vanilla (Pillsbury) *Rich'n Easy* | ⅟₁₂ pkg. | 30 |
| White: | | |
| (Betty Crocker) fluffy | ⅟₁₂ pkg. | 40 |

22

| Food and Description | Measure or Quantity | Sodium (mgs.) |
|---|---|---|
| (Betty Crocker) sour cream, creamy | ¹⁄₁₂ pkg. | 100 |
| (Pillsbury) fluffy | ¹⁄₁₂ pkg. | 65 |

## CAKE MIX:
Regular:
Angel Food:
(Betty Crocker):

| | | |
|---|---|---|
| Chocolate | ¹⁄₁₂ pkg. | 275 |
| One Step | ¹⁄₁₂ pkg. | 250 |
| Traditional | ¹⁄₁₂ pkg. | 140 |
| (Duncan Hines) | ¹⁄₁₂ pkg. | 119 |
| *(Pillsbury) raspberry | ¹⁄₁₂ of cake | 300 |

Applesauce raisin (Betty Crocker)

| | | |
|---|---|---|
| Snackin' Cake | ¹⁄₉ pkg. | 250 |
| *Applesauce spice (Pillsbury) | ¹⁄₁₂ of cake | 300 |

Banana:

| | | |
|---|---|---|
| *(Betty Crocker) Supermoist | ¹⁄₁₂ of cake | 255 |
| *(Pillsbury) Pillsbury Plus | ¹⁄₁₂ of cake | 200 |

Banana walnut (Betty Crocker)

| | | |
|---|---|---|
| Snackin' Cake | ¹⁄₉ pkg. | 260 |
| *Boston cream (Pillsbury) Bundt | ¹⁄₁₆ of cake | 305 |

*Butter (Pillsbury):

| | | |
|---|---|---|
| Pillsbury Plus | ¹⁄₁₂ of cake | 345 |
| Streusel Swirl, rich | ¹⁄₁₆ of cake | 235 |

*Butter Brickle (Betty Crocker)

| | | |
|---|---|---|
| Supermoist | ¹⁄₁₂ of cake | 265 |

*Butter pecan (Betty Crocker)

| | | |
|---|---|---|
| Supermoist | ¹⁄₁₂ of cake | 250 |

*Carrot (Betty Crocker)

| | | |
|---|---|---|
| Supermoist | ¹⁄₁₂ of cake | 200 |

*Carrot'n spice (Pillsbury)

| | | |
|---|---|---|
| Pillsbury Plus | ¹⁄₁₂ of cake | 330 |

*Cheesecake:

| | | |
|---|---|---|
| (Jell-O) | ¹⁄₈ of 8" cake | 351 |
| (Royal) | ¹⁄₈ of cake | 442 |

*Cherry chip (Betty Crocker)

| | | |
|---|---|---|
| Supermoist | ¹⁄₁₂ of cake | 265 |

Chocolate:
(Betty Crocker):

| | | |
|---|---|---|
| *Pudding | ¹⁄₆ of cake | 255 |

Snackin' Cake:

| | | |
|---|---|---|
| Almond | ¹⁄₉ pkg. | 215 |
| Fudge Chip | ¹⁄₉ pkg. | 205 |

Stir 'N Frost:

| | | |
|---|---|---|
| With chocolate frosting | ¹⁄₆ pkg. | 200 |
| Fudge, with vanilla frosting | ¹⁄₆ pkg. | 250 |

| Food and Description | Measure or Quantity | Sodium (mgs.) |
|---|---|---|
| *Supermoist:* | | |
| *Fudge | 1/12 of cake | 450 |
| *Milk | 1/12 of cake | 290 |
| *(Pillsbury): | | |
| *Bundt:* | | |
| Fudge nut crown | 1/16 of cake | 290 |
| Fudge, tunnel | 1/16 of cake | 315 |
| Macaroon | 1/16 of cake | 305 |
| *Pillsbury Plus:* | | |
| Fudge, dark | 1/12 of cake | 440 |
| Fudge, marble | 1/12 of cake | 300 |
| *Streusel Swirl*, German | 1/16 of cake | 290 |
| *Cinnamon (Pillsbury) *Streusel Swirl* | 1/16 of cake | 200 |
| Coconut pecan (Betty Crocker) *Snackin' Cake* | 1/9 pkg. | 255 |
| Coffee cake: | | |
| *(Aunt Jemima) | 1/8 of cake | 34 |
| *(Pillsbury): | | |
| Apple cinnamon | 1/8 of cake | 155 |
| Butter pecan | 1/8 of cake | 335 |
| Cinnamon streusel | 1/8 of cake | 225 |
| Date nut (Betty Crocker) *Snackin' cake* | 1/9 pkg. | 265 |
| Devil's food: | | |
| *(Betty Crocker) *Supermoist* | 1/12 of cake | 425 |
| (Duncan Hines) deluxe | 1/12 pkg. | 363 |
| *(Pillsbury) *Pillsbury Plus* | 1/12 of cake | 405 |
| Fudge (See Chocolate) | | |
| Golden chocolate chip (Betty Crocker) *Snackin' Cake* | 1/9 pkg. | 255 |
| Lemon: | | |
| (Betty Crocker): | | |
| *Chiffon | 1/12 of cake | 190 |
| *Stir 'N Frost*, with lemon frosting | 1/12 pkg. | 270 |
| *Supermoist* | 1/12 of cake | 260 |
| *(Pillsbury): | | |
| *Bundt*, tunnel of | 1/16 of cake | 295 |
| *Streusel Swirl* | 1/16 of cake | 310 |
| *Lemon blueberry (Pillsbury) *Bundt* | 1/16 of cake | 270 |
| Marble: | | |
| *(Betty Crocker) *Supermoist* | 1/12 of cake | 255 |
| *(Pillsbury): | | |
| *Bundt*, supreme, ring | 1/16 of cake | 265 |
| *Streusel Swirl*, fudge | 1/16 of cake | 200 |

| Food and Description | Measure or Quantity | Sodium (mgs.) |
|---|---|---|
| *Oats'n brown sugar (Pillsbury) | | |
|    *Pillsbury Plus* | ¹⁄₁₂ of cake | 305 |
| *Orange (Betty Crocker) | | |
|    *Supermoist* | ¹⁄₁₂ of cake | 280 |
| Pound: | | |
|    *(Betty Crocker) golden | ¹⁄₁₂ of cake | 155 |
|    *(Pillsbury) *Bundt* | ¹⁄₁₆ of cake | 260 |
| Spice (Betty Crocker): | | |
|    *Snackin' cake*, raisin | ⅑ pkg. | 250 |
|    *Stir N' Frost*, with | | |
|      vanilla frosting | ⅙ of cake | 305 |
|    *Supermoist* | ¹⁄₁₂ of cake | 260 |
| Strawberry: | | |
|    *(Betty Crocker) *Supermoist* | ¹⁄₁₂ of cake | 260 |
|    *(Pillsbury) *Pillsbury Plus* | ¹⁄₁₂ of cake | 300 |
| *Upside down (Betty Crocker) | | |
|    pineapple | ⅑ of cake | 215 |
| White: | | |
|    *(Betty Crocker): | | |
|      *Stir 'N Frost*, with chocolate | | |
|       frosting | ⅙ of cake | 235 |
|      *Supermoist* | ¹⁄₁₂ of cake | 275 |
|    (Duncan Hines) deluxe | ¹⁄₁₂ of pkg. | 251 |
|    *(Pillsbury) *Pillsbury Plus* | ¹⁄₁₂ of cake | 295 |
| Yellow: | | |
|    *(Betty Crocker) *Supermoist* | ¹⁄₁₂ of cake | 270 |
|    (Duncan Hines) deluxe | ¹⁄₁₂ of pkg. | 271 |
|    *(Pillsbury) *Pillsbury Plus* | ¹⁄₁₂ of cake | 300 |
| *Dietetic: | | |
|    Chocolate (Dia-Mel) | ¹⁄₁₀ of cake | 110 |
|    Lemon (Dia-Mel) | ¹⁄₁₀ of cake | 75 |
|    Pound (Dia-Mel) | ¹⁄₁₀ of cake | 75 |
|    White (Estee) | ¹⁄₁₀ of cake | 75 |
| **CANDY, REGULAR:** | | |
| Almond, chocolate covered | | |
|    (Hershey's) *Golden Almond* | 1 oz. | 17 |
| Almond, Jordan | 1 oz. | 6 |
| *Baby Ruth* | 1.8-oz. piece | 102 |
| *Butterfinger* | 1.6-oz. bar | 68 |
| *Butternut* (Hollywood Brands) | 2¼-oz. piece | 120 |
| Candy corn | 1 oz. | 60 |
| *Caramel Nip* (Pearson) | 1 piece | 34 |
| Chocolate bar: | | |
|    *Crunch* (Nestlé) | 1¹⁄₁₆-oz. bar | 50 |
|    Milk: | | |
|      (Hershey's) | 1.2-oz. bar | 29 |
|      (Hershey's) | 4-oz. bar | 97 |

| Food and Description | Measure or Quantity | Sodium (mgs.) |
|---|---|---|
| (Nestlé) | .35-oz. bar | 5 |
| (Nestlé) | 1¹⁄₁₆-oz. bar | 15 |
| *Special Dark* (Hershey's) | 1.05-oz. bar | 1 |
| *Special Dark* (Hershey's) | 4-oz. bar | 6 |
| Chocolate bar with almonds: | | |
| (Hershey's) milk | .35-oz. bar | 8 |
| (Hershey's) milk | 1.15-oz. bar | 28 |
| (Nestlé) | 1-oz. | 20 |
| *Chocolate Parfait* (Pearson) | 1 piece | 3 |
| *Coffee Nip* (Pearson) | 1 piece | 17 |
| *Coffioca* (Pearson) | 1 piece | 5 |
| Gumdrops | 1 oz. | 10 |
| Halvah (Sahadi) | 1 oz. | 45 |
| Hard (Jolly Rancher): | | |
| Apple, fire, lemon or watermelon | 1 piece | 5 |
| Butterscotch | 1 piece | 37 |
| Orange | 1 piece | 4 |
| Jelly bean | 1 oz. | 3 |
| *Kisses* (Hershey's) | 1 piece (.2 oz.) | 5 |
| *Kit Kat* | .6-oz. bar | 15 |
| *Krackel Bar* | .35-oz. bar | 16 |
| *Krackel Bar* | 1.2-oz. bar | 55 |
| *Licorice Nips* (Pearson) | 1 piece | 34 |
| *Life Savers*, drop | 1 piece | Tr. |
| *Life Savers*, mint | 1 piece | Tr. |
| Lollipops (Life Savers) | .9-oz. pop | 7 |
| *Mars Bar* (M&M/Mars) | 1.7-oz. serving | 73 |
| Marshmallow | 1 oz. | 11 |
| *Mary Jane* (Miller): | | |
| Small size | ¼ oz. | 4 |
| Large size | 1½-oz. bar | 23 |
| *Milky Way* (M&M/Mars) | 2.1-oz. bar | 113 |
| *Mint Parfait* (Pearson) | 1 piece | 35 |
| *M & M's:* | | |
| Peanut | 1.67-oz. | 28 |
| Plain | 1.69-oz. | 43 |
| *Mr. Goodbar* (Hershey's) | .35-oz. bar | 5 |
| *Mr. Goodbar* (Hershey's) | 1½-oz. bar | 19 |
| *My Buddy* (Tom's) | 1.8-oz. piece | 60 |
| *$100,000 Bar* (Nestle) | 1¼-oz. bar | 50 |
| *Park Avenue* (Tom's) | 1.8-oz. piece | 120 |
| Peanut butter cup (Reese's) | .6-oz. cup | 52 |
| *Peanut Butter Pals* (Tom's) | 1.3-oz. serving | 100 |
| Raisin, chocolate-covered | 1 oz. | 18 |
| *Reese's Pieces* | 1 oz. | 37 |
| *Reggie Bar* | 2-oz. bar | 40 |
| *Rolo* (Hershey's) | 1 piece | 9 |

| Food and Description | Measure or Quantity | Sodium (mgs.) |
|---|---|---|
| *Royals,* mint chocolate (M&M/Mars) | 1.52-oz. pkg. | 37 |
| Sesame Crunch Bar (Sahadi) | ¾-oz. bar | 55 |
| Sesame Tahini (Sahadi) | 1 oz. | 75 |
| *Snickers* (M&M/Mars) | 2-oz. bar | 143 |
| Starburst (M&M/Mars) | 1-oz. serving | 13 |
| *Summit,* bar (M&M/Mars) | .75-oz. | 31 |
| *3 Musketeers* | 2.06-oz.bar | 124 |
| *Tootsie Roll:* | | |
| Chocolate | .23-oz. midgee | 1 |
| Chocolate | ¹⁄₁₆-oz. bar | 4 |
| Chocolate | 1-oz. bar | 6 |
| Flavored | .6-oz. square | 1 |
| Pop, all flavors | .49-oz. pop | 4 |
| Pop drop, all flavors | 4.7-gram piece | 1 |
| *Twix,* cookie bar (M&M/Mars) | 1¾-oz. serving | 95 |
| *Twix,* peanut butter cookie bar (M&M/Mars) | 1¾-oz. serving | 159 |
| *Whatchamacallit* (Hershey's) | 1.15-oz. bar | 132 |
| **CANDY, DIETETIC:** | | |
| Carob bar, *Joan's Natural:* | | |
| Coconut | 3-oz. bar | 117 |
| Fruit & nut | 3-oz. bar | 115 |
| Honey bran | 3-oz. bar | 114 |
| Peanut | 3-oz. bar | 109 |
| Chocolate or chocolate flavored bar (Estee): | | |
| Coconut | 2½-oz. bar | 61 |
| Crunch | 2-oz. bar | 65 |
| Fruit & nut | 2½-oz. bar | 59 |
| Milk | 2½-oz. bar | 68 |
| Toasted bran | 2½-oz. bar | 62 |
| *Estee-ets,* with peanuts (Estee) | 1 piece | 2 |
| Gum drops (Estee) any flavor | 1 piece | 1 |
| Hard candy: | | |
| (Estee) assorted fruit or peppermint | 1 piece | 2 |
| (Louis Sherry) | 1 piece | 2 |
| Mint (Estee) all flavors | 1 piece | 0 |
| Peanut butter cup (Estee) | 1 piece | 10 |
| Raisins, chocolate-covered (Estee) | 1 piece | 2 |
| **CANNELONI** frozen: | | |
| (Stouffer's) cheese in tomato sauce | 9⅛-oz. pkg. | 885 |
| (Weight Watchers) one-compartment, Florentine | 13-oz. meal | 894 |
| **CANTALOUPE,** cubed | ½ cup | 10 |

| Food and Description | Measure or Quantity | Sodium (mgs.) |
|---|---|---|
| **CAP'N CRUNCH,** cereal (Quaker): | | |
| Regular | ¾ cup | 185 |
| Crunchberry | ¾ cup | 166 |
| Peanut butter | ¾ cup | 210 |
| **CAPOCOLLO** (Hormel) | 1 oz. | 273 |
| **CARAWAY SEED** (French's) | 1 tsp. | Tr. |
| **CARNATION-DO-IT-YOURSELF DIET PLAN** | 2 scoops | 110 |
| **CARNATION INSTANT BREAKFAST:** | | |
| Bar: | | |
| Chocolate chip | 1 bar | 180 |
| Chocolate crunch | 1 bar | 145 |
| Peanut butter crunch | 1 bar | 170 |
| Packets: | | |
| Chocolate | 1 packet | 135 |
| Coffee | 1 packet | 130 |
| Strawberry | 1 packet | 195 |
| Vanilla | 1 packet | 135 |
| **CARROT:** | | |
| Raw | 5½″ × 1″ piece | 24 |
| Boiled slices | ½ cup | 25 |
| Canned, regular pack, solids & liq.: | | |
| (Comstock) | ½ cup | 320 |
| (Del Monte) | ½ cup | 265 |
| (Libby's) | ½ cup | 280 |
| (Stokely-Van Camp) sliced | ½ cup | 263 |
| Canned, dietetic pack, solids & liq.: | | |
| (Featherweight) | ½ cup | 30 |
| (Larsen) *Fresh-Lite* | ½ cup | 37 |
| (S&W) *Nutradiet,* slices, green label | ½ cup | 50 |
| Frozen: | | |
| (Birds Eye) whole, baby, deluxe | ⅓ pkg. | 46 |
| (Green Giant) cuts, in butter sauce | ½ cup | 315 |
| (McKenzie) | ⅓ pkg. | 44 |
| **CARROT PUREE** (Larsen) | ½ cup | 33 |
| **CASABA MELLON,** whole | 1-lb. melon | 27 |
| **CASHEW NUT:** | | |
| (Fisher) salted: | | |
| Dry roasted | 1 oz. | 137 |
| Oil roasted | 1 oz. | 137 |
| (Planters) salted: | | |
| Dry roasted | 1 oz. | 222 |
| Oil roasted | 1 oz. | 219 |
| (Tom's) | 1 oz. | 122 |

| Food and Description | Measure or Quantity | Sodium (mgs.) |
|---|---|---|
| **CATFISH,** frozen (Mrs. Paul's) breaded & fried, finger | 4 oz. | 260 |
| **CATSUP:** | | |
| Regular: | | |
| (Del Monte) | 1 T. (.5 oz.) | 181 |
| (Smucker's) | 1 T. | 107 |
| Dietetic or low calorie: | | |
| (Del Monte) No Salt Added | 1 T. | 6 |
| (Featherweight) | 1 T. | 5 |
| (Tillie Lewis) *Tasti Diet* | 1 T. | 6 |
| **CAULIFLOWER:** | | |
| Raw or boiled buds | ½ cup (1.8 oz.) | 6 |
| Frozen: | | |
| (Birds Eye): | | |
| With cheese sauce | ⅓ pkg. | 336 |
| Florets, deluxe | 3⅓-oz. | 18 |
| (Green Giant) in cheese sauce | ½ cup | 450 |
| **CAVIAR,** whole eggs | 1 T. | 352 |
| **CELERY:** | | |
| 1 large outer stalk | 8″ × 1½″ at root end | 50 |
| Diced or cut | ½ cup | 63 |
| Salt (French's) | 1 tsp. | 1505 |
| Seed (French's) | 1 tsp. | 4 |
| **CERVELAT** (Hormel) Viking | 1 oz. | 325 |
| **CHABLIS WINE** (Great Western) | 3 fl. oz. | 31 |
| **CHAMPAGNE** (Great Western) | 3 fl. oz. | 31 |
| **CHARLOTTE RUSSE,** home recipe | 4 oz. | 49 |
| *CHEERIOS*, cereal: | | |
| Regular | 1¼ cups | 330 |
| Honey nut | ¾ cup | 255 |
| **CHEESE:** | | |
| American or cheddar: | | |
| Cube, natural | 1″ cube (.6 oz.) | 119 |
| (Featherweight) low sodium | 1 oz. | 6 |
| *Laughing Cow*, natural | 1 oz. | 227 |
| (Sargento): | | |
| Midget, regular or sharp | 1 oz. | 176 |
| Shredded, non-dairy | 1 oz. | 269 |
| Blue: | | |
| (Frigo) | 1 oz. | 511 |
| (Sargento) cold pack or crumbled | 1 oz. | 396 |
| Brick (Sargento) | 1 oz. | 159 |
| Brie (Sargento) *Danish Danko* | 1 oz. | 282 |
| Burgercheese (Sargento) | 1 oz. | 406 |
| Camembert (Sargento) *Danish Danko* | 1 oz. | 222 |

| Food and Description | Measure or Quantity | Sodium (mgs.) |
|---|---|---|
| Colby: | | |
|   (Featherweight) low sodium | 1 oz. | 4 |
|   (Pauly) low sodium | 1 oz. | 5 |
|   (Sargento) shredded or sliced | 1 oz. | 171 |
| Cottage: | | |
|   Unflavored: | | |
|     (USDA) | 1 oz. | 65 |
|     (Friendship) no salt added | 1 oz. | 7 |
|   Flavored (Breakstone) Chive | 1 T. (.6 oz.) | 64 |
| Cream, plain, unwhipped: | | |
|   *Philadelphia* (Kraft) | 1 oz. | 113 |
| Edam: | | |
|   (House of Gold) | 1 oz. | 204 |
|   *Laughing Cow* | 1 oz. | 227 |
|   (Sargento) | 1 oz. | 274 |
| Farmers: | | |
|   (Friendship) no salt added | 1 oz. | 2 |
|   (Sargento) | 1 oz. | 132 |
| Feta (Sargento) Danish, cups | 1 oz. | 316 |
| Gjetost (Sargento) Norwegian | 1 oz. | 170 |
| Gouda: | | |
|   *Laughing Cow*, natural | 1 oz. | 227 |
|   (Sargento) baby, caraway | | |
|     or smoked | 1 oz. | 232 |
|   *Wispride* | 1 oz. | 298 |
| Gruyere, *Swiss Knight* | 1 oz. | 362 |
| Havarti (Sargento) creamy or | | |
|   60% mild | 1 oz. | 198 |
| Hoop (Friendship) natural | 1 oz. | 3 |
| Hot pepper (Sargento) | 1 oz. | 171 |
| Jarlsberg (Sargento) Norwegian | 1 oz. | 130 |
| Kettle Moraine (Sargento) | 1 oz. | 17 |
| Limburger (Sargento) natural | 1 oz. | 227 |
| Monterey Jack: | | |
|   (Frigo) | 1 oz. | 204 |
|   (Sargento) midget, Longhorn, | | |
|     shredded or sliced | 1 oz. | 152 |
| Mozzarella: | | |
|   (Frigo) part skim milk | 1 oz. | 227 |
|   (Sargento): | | |
|     Bar, rounds, shredded regular | | |
|       or with spices, sliced for | | |
|       pizza or square | 1 oz. | 150 |
|     Whole milk | 1 oz. | 106 |
| Muenster: | | |
|   (Sargento) red rind | 1 oz. | 178 |
|   *Wispride* | 1 oz. | 129 |

| Food and Description | Measure or Quantity | Sodium (mgs.) |
|---|---|---|
| Nibblin Curds (Sargento) | 1 oz. | 176 |
| Parmesan: | | |
| (Frigo): | | |
| Grated | 1 T. | 88 |
| Whole | 1 oz. | 341 |
| (Sargento): | | |
| Grated | 1 T. | 102 |
| Wedge | 1 oz. | 454 |
| Pizza (Sargento) shredded or sliced | 1 oz. | 306 |
| Pot (Sargento) regular, | | |
| French onion or garlic | 1 oz. | Tr. |
| Provolone: | | |
| (Frigo) | 1 oz. | 284 |
| (Sargento) sliced | 1 oz. | 248 |
| Ricotta (Sargento): | | |
| Part skim milk | 1 oz. | 35 |
| Whole milk | 1 oz. | 24 |
| Romano (Sargento) wedge | 1 oz. | 340 |
| Sansoe (Sargento) Danish | 1 oz. | 198 |
| Scamorze (Frigo) | 1 oz. | 227 |
| Semisoft, *Laughing Cow:* | | |
| Babybel | 1 oz. | 227 |
| *Bonbel*, regular or reduced calorie | 1 oz. | 227 |
| String (Sargento) | 1 oz. | 150 |
| Swiss (Sargento) domestic or | | |
| Finland, sliced | 1 oz. | 74 |
| Taco (Sargento) shredded | 1 oz. | 47 |
| **CHEESE FONDUE,** *Swiss Knight* | 1 oz. | 186 |
| **CHEESE FOOD:** | | |
| American or cheddar: | | |
| (Fisher) *Ched-O-Mate* | 1 oz. | 420-450 |
| (Sargento) | 1 oz. | 274 |
| (Weight Watchers) colored | | |
| or white | 1-oz. slice | 533 |
| *Wispride:* | | |
| Regular | 1 oz. | 180 |
| & port wine | 1 oz. | 190 |
| *Cheez-ola* (Fisher): | | |
| Regular | 1 oz. | 400-430 |
| Low sodium | 1 oz. | 150-170 |
| Cracker snack (Sargento) | 1 oz. | 406 |
| Garlic & Herb, *Wispride* | 1 oz. | 180 |
| *Mun-chee* (Pauly) | 1 oz. | 485 |
| Pimiento (Pauly) | .8-oz. slice | 426 |
| *Pizza-mate* (Fisher) | 1 oz. | 330-350 |
| Swiss (Pauly) | .8-oz. slice | 58 |

31

| Food and Description | Measure or Quantity | Sodium (mgs.) |
|---|---|---|
| **CHEESE SPREAD:** | | |
| American or cheddar (Nabisco) *Snack Mate* | 1 tsp. | 65 |
| Blue, *Laughing Cow* | 1 oz. | 312 |
| Cheese'n Bacon (Nabisco) *Snack Mate* | 1 tsp. | 58 |
| Gruyere, *Laughing Cow*, *La Vache Que Rit* | 1 oz. | 312 |
| Pimiento: | | |
| (Nabisco) *Snack Mate* | 1 tsp. | 60 |
| (Price's) | 1 oz. | 335 |
| Provolone, *Laughing Cow* | 1 oz. | 312 |
| Sharp (Pauly) | .8 oz. | 437 |
| Swiss, process (Pauly) | .8 oz. | 391 |
| **CHEESE STRAW,** frozen | 1 piece (6 grams) | 43 |
| **CHERRY, SWEET:** | | |
| Fresh, with stems | ½ cup | 1 |
| Canned, regular pack (Del Monte) pitted, solids & liq.: | ½ cup | <10 |
| Canned, dietetic, solids & liq.: | | |
| (Diet Delight) with pits, water pack | ½ cup | 5 |
| (Featherweight) dark or light | ½ cup | <10 |
| **CHERRY DRINK** (Hi-C): | | |
| Canned | 6 fl. oz. | 4 |
| *Mix | 6 fl. oz. | 23 |
| **CHERRY JELLY:** | | |
| Sweetened (Smucker's) | 1 T. | 3 |
| Dietetic: | | |
| (Featherweight) | 1 T. | 40-50 |
| (Slenderella) | 1 T. | 22 |
| **CHERRY PRESERVE OR JAM:** | | |
| Sweetened (Smucker's) | 1 T. | 6 |
| Dietetic (Dia-Mel; Louis Sherry) | 1 T. | <3 |
| **CHESTNUT,** fresh, in shell | ¼ lb. | 220 |
| **CHEWING GUM,** sweetened or dietetic | 1 piece | Tr. |
| *CHEX*, cereal (Ralston Purina:) | | |
| Rice | 1 cup | 243 |
| Wheat | ⅔ cup | 192 |
| Wheat & raisins | ¾ cup | 216 |
| **CHICKEN:** | | |
| Broiler, cooked, meat only | 3 oz. | 56 |
| Fryer, fried, meat & skin | 3 oz. | 66 |
| Fryer, fried, meat only | 3 oz. | 66 |
| Fryer, fried, a 2½ lb. chicken (weighed with bone before cooking) will give you: | | |

| Food and Description | Measure or Quantity | Sodium (mgs.) |
|---|---|---|
| Dark meat with skin | 4 oz. | 100 |
| Light meat with skin | 4 oz. | 77 |
| Hen & cock: | | |
| Stewed, dark meat only | 3 oz. | 55 |
| Stewed, light meat only | 3 oz. | 41 |
| Stewed, diced | ½ cup | 47 |
| Roaster, roasted, dark or light meat, without skin | 3 oz. | 65 |
| **CHICKEN À LA KING:** | | |
| Home recipe | 1 cup | 760 |
| Canned (Swanson) | ½ of 10½-oz. can | 695 |
| Frozen: | | |
| (Banquet) *Cookin' Bag* | 5-oz. pkg. | 645 |
| (Green Giant) with biscuits | 9-oz. entree | 1545 |
| (Le Menu) | 10¼-oz. dinner | 1170 |
| (Morton) | 5-oz. pkg. | 510 |
| (Stouffer's) with rice | 9½-oz. pkg. | 900 |
| (Weight Watchers) | 9-oz. pkg. | 980 |
| **CHICKEN BOUILLON:** | | |
| (Herb-Ox): | | |
| Cube | 1 cube | 950 |
| Packet | 1 packet | 960 |
| Low sodium (Featherweight) | 1 tsp. | 5 |
| **CHICKEN, BONED, CANNED:** | | |
| (Hormel) breast | 6¾ oz. | 855 |
| (Swanson) chunk: | | |
| Mixin' chicken | 2½ oz. | 225 |
| White | 2½ oz. | 235 |
| Low sodium (Featherweight) | 2½ oz. | 99 |
| **CHICKEN CREAMED,** frozen | | |
| (Stouffer's) | 6½-oz. pkg. | 680 |
| **CHICKEN DINNER OR ENTREE:** | | |
| Canned (Swanson) & dumplings | 7½-oz. serving | 980 |
| Frozen: | | |
| (Banquet): | | |
| American Favorites | 11-oz. dinner | 1831 |
| Extra Helping Dinner: | | |
| & dressing | 19-oz. dinner | 1817 |
| & dumpling | 19-oz. dinner | 1923 |
| Fried | 17-oz. dinner | 2780 |
| (Green Giant): | | |
| Baked: | | |
| In BBQ sauce | 1 meal | 885 |
| Stir fry, cashews | 1 meal | 965 |
| Stir fry, sweet & sour | 1 meal | 585 |
| Twin pouch, brocolli with rice in cheese sauce | 9½-oz. entree | 915 |

| Food and Description | Measure or Quantity | Sodium (mgs.) |
|---|---|---|
| (Le Menu) sweet & sour | 11½-oz. dinner | 960 |
| (Morton): | | |
| Regular: | | |
| Boneless | 10-oz. dinner | 1350 |
| Sliced | 5-oz. pkg. | 810 |
| *Country Table*, fried | 15-oz. dinner | 2180 |
| (Stouffer's): | | |
| Cacciatore, with spaghetti | 11¼-oz. meal | 1135 |
| Divan | 8½-oz. serving | 830 |
| *Lean Cuisine*, glazed with vegetable rice | 8½-oz. serving | 830 |
| (Swanson): | | |
| Regular: | | |
| & dumplings | 7½-oz. meal | 965 |
| Fried, 4-compartment: | | |
| Barbecue flavor | 9¼-oz. dinner | 845 |
| Breast portion | 10¾-oz. dinner | 1425 |
| *Hungry Man:* | | |
| Boneless | 17½-oz. dinner | 1525 |
| Fried, breast | 14-oz. dinner | 2060 |
| Parmigiana | 20-oz. dinner | 2205 |
| (Weight Watchers): | | |
| Cacciatore | 10-oz. serving | 929 |
| Oriental style | 9½-oz. serving | 834 |
| Parmigiana, 2-compartment | 7¾-oz. serving | 734 |
| Sliced in celery sauce, 2-compartment | 8½-oz. serving | 651 |
| Southern fried patty, 2-compartment | 6¾-oz. serving | 788 |
| **CHICKEN, FRIED, FROZEN:** | | |
| (Banquet): | | |
| Assorted | 2-lb. pkg. | 6005 |
| Breast portion | 22-oz. pkg. | 3860 |
| Wings | 27-oz. pkg. | 4904 |
| (Morton) assorted | 2-lb. pkg. | 7925 |
| (Swanson) Plump & Juicy: | | |
| Assorted | 3¼-oz. serving | 655 |
| Breast portions | 3¼-oz. serving | 865 |
| Nibbles | 3¼-oz. serving | 645 |
| Take-out style | 3¼-oz. serving | 730 |
| **CHICKEN & NOODLES,** frozen: | | |
| (Banquet) *Buffet Supper* | 2-lb. pkg. | 5645 |
| (Green Giant) with vegetables | 9-oz. pkg. | 940 |
| (Stouffer's): | | |
| Escalloped | 5¾-oz. serving | 720 |
| Paprikash | 10½-oz. serving | 1325 |

34

| Food and Description | Measure or Quantity | Sodium (mgs.) |
|---|---|---|
| **CHICKEN NUGGETS,** frozen | | |
| (Banquet) breaded & fried | 12-oz. pkg. | 676 |
| **CHICKEN, PACKAGED** (Eckrich) | | |
| breast, sliced | 1-oz. slice | 210 |
| **CHICKEN PATTY,** frozen (Banquet) | | |
| breaded & fried | 12-oz. pkg. | 604 |
| **CHICKEN PIE,** frozen: | | |
| (Banquet) regular | 8-oz. pie | 1027 |
| (Morton) | 8-oz. pie | 1246 |
| (Stouffer's) | 10-oz. pie | 1530 |
| (Swanson): | | |
| Regular | 8-oz. pie | 850 |
| *Hungry Man* | 16-oz. pie | 1680 |
| (Van de Kamp's) | 7½-oz. pie | 890 |
| **CHICKEN SALAD** (Carnation) | ¼ of 7½-oz. | |
| | can | 230 |
| **CHICKEN SOUP** (See SOUP, Chicken) | | |
| **CHICKEN SPREAD:** | | |
| (Hormel) regular | 1 oz. | 304 |
| (Swanson) | 1 oz. | 140 |
| (Underwood) chunky | 1 oz. | 240 |
| **CHICKEN STEW,** canned: | | |
| Regular: | | |
| (Libby's) with dumplings | 8 oz. | 976 |
| (Swanson) | 7⅝-oz. | 960 |
| Dietetic: | | |
| (Dia-Mel) | 8-oz. can | 65 |
| (Featherweight) | 7½-oz. | 53 |
| **CHICKEN STICKS,** frozen (Banquet) | 12-oz. pkg. | 664 |
| **CHICKEN STOCK BASE** (French's) | 1 tsp. | 475 |
| **CHICK PEAS,** dry | ½ cup | 26 |
| **CHILI OR CHILI CON CARNE:** | | |
| Canned, regular pack: | | |
| Beans only: | | |
| (Hormel) in sauce | 5 oz. | 453 |
| (Van Camp) Mexican style | 1 cup | 900 |
| With beans: | | |
| (Hormel) hot | 7½-oz. serving | 1121 |
| (Libby's) | 7½-oz. serving | 810 |
| (Old El Paso) | 1 cup | 907 |
| (Swanson) | 7¾-oz. serving | 1100 |
| Without beans | | |
| (Hormel) regular | ½ of 15-oz. can | 1012 |
| Canned, dietetic pack: | | |
| (Dia-Mel) with beans | 8-oz. serving | 50 |
| (Featherweight) with beans | 7½-oz. | 85 |

| Food and Description | Measure or Quantity | Sodium (mgs.) |
|---|---|---|
| Frozen, with beans (Weight Watchers) one-compartment | 10-oz. pkg. | 822 |
| **CHILI MAC** (Hormel) | | |
| *Short Orders* | 7½-oz.can | 1418 |
| **CHILI SAUCE:** | | |
| (Del Monte) | ¼ cup (2 oz.) | 835 |
| (Ortega) green | 1 oz. | 175 |
| (Featherweight) dietetic | 1 T. | 10 |
| **CHILI SEASONING MIX:** | | |
| *(Durkee) | 1 cup | 979 |
| (French's) *Chili-O* | 1¾-oz. pkg. | 3780 |
| **CHOCO-DILE** (Hostess) | 2-oz. piece | 280 |
| **CHOCOLATE, BAKING:** | | |
| (Baker's): | | |
| Bitter or unsweetened | 1 oz. | 1 |
| Semi-sweet, chips | ¼ cup | 9 |
| Sweetened, *German* | 1 oz. | 3 |
| (Hershey's): | | |
| Bitter or unsweetened | 1 oz. | Tr. |
| Sweetened: | | |
| Dark chips, regular or mini | 1 oz. | 65 |
| Milk, chips | 1 oz. | 31 |
| Semi-sweet, chips | 1 oz. | 3 |
| (Nestlé): | | |
| Bitter or unsweetened, *Choco-bake* | 1-oz. packet | 5 |
| Sweet or semi-sweet, morsels | 1 oz. | <5 |
| **CHOCOLATE ICE CREAM** (See ICE CREAM, Chocolate) | | |
| **CHOCOLATE SYRUP** (See SYRUP, Chocolate) | | |
| **CHOP SUEY**, frozen: | | |
| (Banquet) beef: | | |
| *Buffet Supper* | 2-lb. pkg. | 5336 |
| *Cookin' Bag* | 7-oz. bag | 1140 |
| Dinner | 12-oz. dinner | 1802 |
| (Stouffer's) beef with rice | 12-oz. pkg. | 2040 |
| **\*CHOP SUEY SEASONING MIX** (Durkee) | 1¾ cups | 5582 |
| **CHOWDER** (See SOUP, Chowder) | | |
| **CHOW MEIN:** | | |
| Canned: | | |
| (Chun King) chicken | 8-oz. serving | 806 |
| (La Choy): | | |
| Regular: | | |
| Beef | ¾ cup | 1000 |

| Food and Description | Measure or Quantity | Sodium (mgs.) |
|---|---|---|
| Chicken | ¾ cup | 990 |
| Meatless | ¾ cup | 720 |
| Shrimp | ¾ cup | 855 |
| Bi-pack: | | |
| Beef | ¾ cup | 750 |
| Chicken | ¾ cup | 635 |
| Pork | ¾ cup | 1120 |
| Vegetable | ¾ cup | 790 |
| Frozen: | | |
| (Banquet) chicken: | | |
| *Buffet Supper* | 2-lb. pkg. | 4981 |
| Dinner | 12-oz. dinner | 2268 |
| (Green Giant) chicken | 9-oz. entree | 1075 |
| (La Choy): | | |
| Chicken | 11-oz. dinner | 356 |
| Shrimp | 11-oz. entree | 1600 |
| (Stouffer's) *Lean Cuisine* | 11¼-oz. dinner | 1155 |
| **CHOW MEIN** Seasoning Mix | | |
| (Kikkoman) | 1⅛-oz. pkg. | 3 |
| **CINNAMON, GROUND** (French's) | 1 tsp. | Tr. |
| **CITRON, CANDIED** | 1 oz. | 82 |
| ***CITRUS BERRY BLEND***, | | |
| dietic (Sunkist) | 8 fl. oz. | 20 |
| **CITRUS COOLER DRINK,** canned | | |
| (Hi-C) | 6 fl. oz. | 94 |
| **CLAM:** | | |
| Raw, all kinds, meat only | 1 cup (8 oz.) | 465 |
| Frozen (Mrs. Paul's) fried | 2½-oz. serving | 385 |
| ***CLAMATO COCKTAIL*** (Mott's) | 6 fl. oz. | 815 |
| **CLARET WINE** (Gold Seal) | 3 fl. oz. | 3 |
| **CLOVES** (French's) | 1 tsp. | 4 |
| **COBBLER,** frozen | | |
| (Weight Watchers): | | |
| Apple | 4⅜-oz. serving | 195 |
| Black Cherry | 4⅜-oz. serving | 185 |
| **COCOA:** | | |
| Dry, unsweetened (Hershey's) | 1 T. | 1 |
| Mix, regular: | | |
| (Alba '66) instant, all flavors | 1 envelope | 89 |
| (Carnation) all flavors | 1-oz. pkg. | 120 |
| (Hershey's): | | |
| Hot | 1 oz. | 159 |
| Instant | 3 T. | 44 |
| (Nestlé) | 1¼ oz. | 110 |
| (Ovaltine) hot'n rich | 1 oz. | 183 |
| *Swiss Miss,* regular | 6 fl. oz. | 110 |

| Food and Description | Measure or Quantity | Sodium (mgs.) |
|---|---|---|
| Mix, dietetic: | | |
| (Carnation) *70 Calorie* | ¾-oz. packet | 125 |
| (Estee) | 6 fl. oz. | 75 |
| (Ovaltine) hot, reduced calorie | .45-oz. pkg. | 50 |
| *COCOA KRISPIES,* cereal | | |
| (Kellogg's) | ¾ cup | 195 |
| *COCOA PUFFS,* cereal | | |
| (General Mills) | 1 oz. | 205 |
| **COCONUT:** | | |
| Fresh, meat only | 2″ × 2″ × ½″ piece | 10 |
| Grated or shredded, loosely packed | ½ cup | 15 |
| Dried: | | |
| (Baker's): | | |
| *Angel Flake,* bag | ⅓ cup | 73 |
| Cookie | ⅓ cup | 109 |
| Premium shred | ⅓ cup | 84 |
| Southern style | ⅓ cup | 5 |
| (Durkee) shredded | ¼ cup | 5 |
| *COCO WHEATS,* cereal | 1 T. | 3 |
| **COD:** | | |
| Broiled | 4 oz. | 125 |
| Frozen (Van de Kamp's) *Today's Catch* | 4 oz. | 154 |
| **COFFEE:** | | |
| Regular | 6 fl. oz. | Tr. |
| Decaffeinated: | | |
| *Brim,* regular or electric perk | 6 fl. oz. | 5 |
| *Decaf; Néscafé | 6 fl. oz. | <10 |
| *Sanka* regular or electric perk | 6 fl. oz. | 1 |
| Instant: | | |
| *Mellow roast | 6 fl. oz. | 2 |
| *Sunrise | 6 fl. oz. | <10 |
| *Mix (General Foods) | | |
| *International Coffee:* | | |
| Café Amaretto | 6 fl. oz. | 25 |
| Café François, Irish Mocha mint or Swiss Mint | 6 fl. oz. | 24 |
| Café Vienna | 6 fl. oz. | 93 |
| Orange Capuccino | 6 fl. oz. | 98 |
| **COFFEE CAKE** (see CAKE, Coffee) | | |
| *COFFEE SOUTHERN* | 1 fl. oz. | Tr. |
| **COLA SOFT DRINK** | | |
| (See SOFT DRINK, Cola) | | |
| **COLD DUCK WINE** | | |
| (Great Western) pink | 3 fl. oz. | 31 |
| **COLESLAW,** solids & liq., made with mayonnaise-type salad dressing | 1 cup | 148 |

| Food and Description | Measure or Quantity | Sodium (mgs.) |
|---|---|---|
| **COLLARDS:** | | |
| Leaves & stems cooked drained | 4 oz. | 28 |
| Canned (Sunshine) chopped, solids & liq. | ½ cup | 378 |
| Frozen, chopped: | | |
| (Birds Eye) | ⅓ pkg. | 45 |
| (McKenzie) | ⅓ pkg. | 25 |
| **COMPLETE CEREAL** (Elam's) | 1 oz. | 109 |
| **CONCORD WINE:** | | |
| (Gold Seal) | 3 fl. oz. | 125 |
| (Pleasant Valley) red | 3 fl. oz. | 90 |
| **COOKIE, REGULAR:** | | |
| *Almond Windmill* (Nabisco) | 1 piece | 47 |
| Animal: | | |
| (Dixie Belle) | 1 piece | 7 |
| (Nabisco) *Barnum's Animals* | 1 piece | 12 |
| (Ralston) | 1 piece | 7 |
| (Tom's) | 1.7 oz | 190 |
| Apple (Pepperidge Farm) | 1 piece | 50 |
| Apple Spice (Pepperidge Farm) | 1 piece | 26 |
| Apricot Raspberry (Pepperidge Farm) | 1 piece | 26 |
| Assortment (Pepperidge Farm): | | |
| Butter | 1 piece | 27 |
| *Champagne* | 1 piece | 18 |
| Chocolate lace & Pirouette | 1 piece | 18 |
| *Marseilles* | 1 piece | 25 |
| *Seville* | 1 piece | 25 |
| *Southport* | 1 piece | 35 |
| *Bordeaux* (Pepperidge Farm) | 1 piece | 23 |
| Brown edge wafer (Nabisco) | 1 piece | 20 |
| Brownie: | | |
| (Hostess) | 1.25-oz. piece | 76 |
| (Pepperidge Farm) chocolate nut | .4-oz. piece | 27 |
| (Sara Lee) frozen | ⅛ of 13-oz. pkg. | 108 |
| *Brussles* (Pepperidge Farm) | 1 piece | 32 |
| *Brussles Mint* (Pepperidge Farm) | 1 piece | 40 |
| Butter (Nabisco) | 1 piece | 17 |
| *Buttercup* (Keebler) | 1 piece | 30 |
| *Cappucino* (Pepperidge Farm) | 1 piece | 20 |
| Caramel peanut log (Nabisco) *Heyday* | 1 piece | 35 |
| *Chessman* (Pepperidge Farm) | 1 piece | 26 |
| Chocolate & chocolate-covered: (Nabisco): | | |
| Famous wafer | 1 piece | 29 |
| *Pinwheel*, cake | 1 piece | 30 |

39

| Food and Description | Measure or Quantity | Sodium (mgs.) |
|---|---|---|
| Snap | 1 piece | 14 |
| Chocolate chip: | | |
| (Nabisco): | | |
| *Chips Ahoy!* | 1 piece | 31 |
| Chocolate | 1 piece | 16 |
| (Pepperidge Farm): | | |
| Regular size | 1 piece | 30 |
| Large size | 1 piece | 80 |
| (Tom's) | 1½ oz. | 110 |
| Cinnamon Sugar | | |
| (Pepperidge Farm) | 1 piece | 37 |
| Coconut: | | |
| (Keebler) chocolate drop | 1 piece | 41 |
| (Nabisco) bar, *Bakers Bonus* | 1 piece | 34 |
| Coconut Granola | | |
| (Pepperidge Farm) | 1 piece | 27 |
| Creme Stick (Dutch Twin) | | |
| chocolate coated | 1 piece | 3 |
| Date Nut Granola | | |
| (Pepperidge Farm) | 1 piece | 32 |
| Date Pecan (Pepperidge Farm) | 1 piece | 20 |
| Fig bar: | | |
| (Keebler) | 1 piece | 84 |
| Nabisco) *Fig Newtons* | 1 piece | 97 |
| (Tom's) | 1.8 oz. | 130 |
| Gingerman (Pepperidge Farm) | 1 piece | 25 |
| Gingersnaps (Nabisco) old fashioned | 1 piece | 41 |
| Granola (Pepperidge Farm) large | 1 piece | 85 |
| Hazelnut (Pepperidge Farm) | 1 piece | 57 |
| Ladyfinger | 3¼" × 1⅜" × 1⅛" | 8 |
| Lemon nut (Pepperidge Farm) | 1 piece | 60 |
| *Lido* (Pepperidge Farm) | 1 piece | 42 |
| Macaroon, coconut (Nabisco) | 1 piece | 17 |
| Marshmallow (Nabisco): | | |
| *Mallomars* | 1 piece | 19 |
| Puffs, cocoa covered | 1 piece | 25 |
| Sandwich | 1 piece | 22 |
| *Twirls* cakes | 1 piece | 32 |
| *Milano* (Pepperidge Farm) | 1 piece | 26 |
| *Mint Milano* (Pepperidge Farm) | 1 piece | 35 |
| Molasses Crisp (Pepperidge Farm) | 1 piece | 25 |
| *Nilla* wafer (Nabisco) | 1 piece | 12 |
| Oatmeal: | | |
| (Keebler) old fashion | 1 piece | 83 |
| (Pepperidge Farm): | | |
| Irish | 1 piece | 40 |
| Large | 1 piece | 105 |

| Food and Description | Measure or Quantity | Sodium (mgs.) |
|---|---|---|
| Raisin | 1 piece | 57 |
| *Orange Milano* (Pepperidge Farm) | 1 piece | 35 |
| *Orleans* (Pepperidge Farm) | 1 piece | 10 |
| Peanut & peanut butter (Nabisco): | | |
| Creme pattie | 1 piece | 18 |
| *Nutter Butter* | 1 piece | 57 |
| Pecan Sandies (Keebler) | 1 piece | 52 |
| Raisin | 1 oz. | 15 |
| Raisin (Nabisco) fruit biscuit | 1 piece | 19 |
| Raisin Bran (Pepperidge Farm) | 1 piece | 27 |
| Sandwich: | | |
| (Keebler) *Pitter Patter* | 1 piece | 117 |
| (Nabisco): | | |
| *Cameo*, creme | 1 piece | 49 |
| *Oreo* | 1 piece | 49 |
| Vanilla, *Cookie Break* | 1 piece | 34 |
| Shortbread or shortcake: | | |
| (Nabisco): | | |
| *Lorna Doone* | 1 piece | 39 |
| Pecan | 1 piece | 44 |
| (Pepperidge Farm) | 1 piece | 43 |
| *Social Tea*, biscuit (Nabisco) | 1 piece | 18 |
| Spiced wafers (Nabisco) | 1 piece | 58 |
| *St. Moritz* (Pepperidge Farm) | 1 piece | 23 |
| Sugar cookie (Nabisco) rings, *Bakers Bonus* | 1 piece | 47 |
| Sugar wafer: | | |
| (Dutch Twin) any flavor | 1 piece | 2 |
| (Keebler) *Krisp Kreem* | 1 piece | 14 |
| (Nabisco) *Biscos* | 1 piece | 5 |
| Sunflower Raisin (Pepperidge Farm) | 1 piece | 25 |
| Tahiti (Pepperidge Farm) | 1 piece | 25 |
| Vanilla wafer (Keebler) | 1 piece | 18 |
| *Zanzibar* (Pepperidge Farm) | 1 piece | 13 |
| **COOKIE, DIETETIC** (Estee): | | |
| Chocolate Chip | 1 piece | 5 |
| Coconut | 1 piece | <5 |
| Oatmeal raisin | 1 piece | <5 |
| Sandwich duplex | 1 piece | 5 |
| Wafer, chocolate covered | 1 piece | 10 |
| *COOKIE CRISP*, cereal: | | |
| Chocolate | 1 cup | 188 |
| Vanilla | 1 cup | 200 |
| ***COOKIE DOUGH:** | | |
| Refrigerated (Pillsbury): | | |
| Chocolate chip | 1 cookie | 42 |
| Peanut butter | 1 cookie | 63 |

41

| Food and Description | Measure or Quantity | Sodium (mgs.) |
|---|---|---|
| Sugar | 1 cookie | 57 |
| Frozen (Rich's): | | |
| Chocolate chip | 1 cookie | 120 |
| Oatmeal | 1 cookie | 90 |
| Peanut butter | 1 cookie | 189 |
| **\*COOKIE MIX:** | | |
| Regular: | | |
| Brownie: | | |
| (Betty Crocker): | | |
| Fudge, regular size | 1/16 pan | 100 |
| Golden supreme, family size | 1/24 pan | 105 |
| Walnut, family size | 1/24 pan | 85 |
| (Duncan Hines) | 1/24 pan | 88 |
| (Nestlé) | 1/23 pkg. | 100 |
| (Pillsbury) fudge, regular size | 2" sq. (1/16 pkg.) | 95 |
| Chocolate chip: | | |
| (Betty Crocker) *Big Batch* | 1 cookie | 47 |
| (Duncan Hines) | 1/36 pkg. | 42 |
| (Quaker) | 1 cookie | 70 |
| Macaroon, coconut | | |
| (Betty Crocker) | 1/24 of pkg. | 15 |
| Oatmeal: | | |
| (Betty Crocker) *Big Batch* | 1 cookie | 50 |
| (Duncan Hines) raisin | 1 cookie | 31 |
| (Nestle) raisin | 1 cookie | 43 |
| (Quaker) | 1 cookie | 71 |
| Peanut butter (Duncan Hines) | 1/36 pkg. | 57 |
| Sugar: | | |
| (Betty Crocker) *Big Batch* | 1 cookie | 47 |
| (Duncan Hines) golden | 1 cookie | 33 |
| Dietetic (Estee) brownie | 2" × 2" piece | 15 |
| **CORN:** | | |
| Fresh, on the cob, boiled | 5" × 1¾" ear | Tr. |
| Canned, regular pack, solids & liq.: | | |
| (Comstock) cream style | ½ cup | 350 |
| (Del Monte) | | |
| Cream style, golden | ½ cup | 355 |
| Whole kernel, vacuum pack | ½ cup | 355 |
| (Green Giant): | | |
| Cream style | 4¼ oz. | 320 |
| Whole kernel | 4¼ oz. | 270 |
| Whole kernel, *Mexicorn* | 3½ oz. | 335 |
| (Larsen) *Freshlike*, whole kernel, vacuum pack | ½ cup | 260 |
| (Le Sueur) whole kernel | 4¼-oz. serving | 285 |
| (Libby's): | | |
| Cream style | ½ cup | 295 |

| Food and Description | Measure or Quantity | Sodium (mgs.) |
|---|---|---|
| Whole kernel | ½ cup | 264 |
| (Stokely-Van Camp): | | |
| Cream style | ½ cup | 383 |
| Whole kernel | ½ cup | 290 |
| Canned, dietetic pack, solids & liq.: | | |
| (Del Monte) No Salt Added | ½ cup | <10 |
| (Diet Delight) | ½ cup | 5 |
| (Featherweight) whole kernel | ½ cup | <10 |
| (Larsen) *Fresh-Lite* | ½ cup | 6 |
| (S&W) *Nutradiet* | ½ cup | <10 |
| Frozen: | | |
| (Birds Eye): | | |
| On the cob: | | |
| *Farmside* | 4.4-oz. ear | 4 |
| *Little Ears* | 2.3-oz. ear | 2 |
| Whole kernel | ⅓ pkg. | 3 |
| Whole kernel in butter sauce | ⅓ pkg. | 178 |
| (Green Giant): | | |
| On the cob | 5½" ear | 20 |
| On the cob, *Nibbler* | 3" ear | 10 |
| Whole kernel, *Niblets,* golden, in butter sauce | ½ cup | 280 |
| (McKenzie) on the cob | 5" ear | 4 |
| **CORNBREAD:** | | |
| Home recipe: | | |
| Corn pone | 4 oz. | 449 |
| Spoon bread | 4 oz. | 547 |
| *Mix: | | |
| (Aunt Jemima) | ⅙ pkg. | 600 |
| (Pillsbury) *Ballard* | ⅛ pkg. | 570 |
| **\*CORN DOGS,** frozen: | | |
| (Hormel) | 1 piece | 656 |
| (Oscar Mayer) | 4-oz. piece | 1282 |
| **CORNED BEEF:** | | |
| Cooked, boneless, medium fat | 4 oz. | 1973 |
| Canned, regular pack, (Libby's) | ⅓ of 7-oz. can | 720 |
| Canned, dietetic (Featherweight) loaf | 2½ oz. | 54 |
| Packaged: | | |
| (Eckrich) sliced | 1-oz. slice | 340 |
| (Oscar Mayer) jellied loaf | 1-oz. slice | 285 |
| **CORNED BEEF HASH:** | | |
| Canned: | | |
| (Libby's) | ⅓ of 24-oz. can | 1330 |
| Mary Kitchen (Hormel) | 7½-oz. serving | 1386 |
| Frozen (Banquet) | 10-oz. dinner | 1752 |

| Food and Description | Measure or Quantity | Sodium (mgs.) |
|---|---|---|
| **CORNED BEEF SPREAD** | | |
| (Underwood) | 2¼ oz. | 605 |
| **CORN FLAKE CRUMBS** (Kellogg's) | ¼ cup | 285 |
| **CORN FLAKES,** cereal: | | |
| (Featherweight) low sodium | 1¼ cups | 10 |
| (General Mills) *Country* | 1 cup | 310 |
| (Kellogg's) *Honey & Nut* or | | |
| sugar frosted | ¾ cup | 190 |
| (Post) *Post Toasties* | 1¼ cups | 229 |
| (Ralston Purina): | | |
| Regular | 1 cup | 267 |
| Sugar frosted | ¾ cup | 179 |
| **CORN MEAL:** | | |
| Bolted (Aunt Jemima/Quaker) | 3 T. | Tr. |
| Degermed | ¼ cup | Tr. |
| Mix (Aunt Jemima) bolted white | ⅙ cup | 337 |
| *CORN POPS,* cereal (Kellog's) | 1 cup | 95 |
| **CORNSTARCH** (Argo; Kingsford's; | | |
| Duryea) | 1 tsp. | Tr. |
| **CORN SYRUP** (See SYRUP, Corn) | | |
| **COUGH DROP** (Beech-Nut) | 1 drop | Tr. |
| *COUNT CHOCULA,* cereal | | |
| (General Mills) | 1 oz. (1 cup) | 205 |
| **CRAB,** canned, drained | 1 cup | 1600 |
| **CRAB APPLE** | ¼ lb. | 1 |
| **CRAB APPLE JELLY** (Smucker's) | 1 T. | 3 |
| **CRAB, DEVILED,** frozen | | |
| (Mrs. Paul's) breaded & fried, | | |
| regular | 3-oz. piece | 385 |
| **CRAB IMPERIAL,** home recipe | 1 cup | 1602 |
| **CRACKER, PUFFS & CHIPS:** | | |
| Arrowroot biscuit (Nabisco) | 1 piece | 11 |
| Bacon-flavored thins (Nabisco) | 1 piece | 32 |
| *Bacon Nips* | 1 oz. | 700 |
| Bacon toast (Keebler) | 1 piece | 28 |
| Bran wafer (Featherweight) | 1 piece | <1 |
| *Bugles* (Tom's) | 1 oz. | 300 |
| Cheese flavored: | | |
| *Cheddar Bitz* (Frito-Lay) | 1 oz. | 239 |
| Cheddar sticks (Flavor Tree) | 1 oz. | 445 |
| Cheese Bites (Tom's) | 1½ oz. | 540 |
| *Chee.Tos,* crunchy | 1 oz. | 172 |
| *Cheez Balls* (Planters) | 1 oz. | 301 |
| *Cheez Curls* (Planters) | 1 oz. | 301 |
| Corn Cheese (Tom's): | | |
| Crunchy | 1 oz. | 170 |
| Puffed, baked | 1 oz. | 260 |

| Food and Description | Measure or Quantity | Sodium (mgs.) |
|---|---|---|
| *Nachips, Old El Paso* | 1 oz. | 193 |
| *Nips* (Nabisco) | 1 piece | 19 |
| (Ralston) | 1 piece | 10 |
| *Tid-Bit* (Nabisco) | 1 oz. | 15 |
| Twists (Bachman) baked | 1 oz. | 150 |
| *Chicken in a Biskit* (Nabisco) | 1 piece | 19 |
| *Chippers* (Nabisco) | 1 piece | 48 |
| *Chipsters* (Nabisco) | 1 piece | 8 |
| Club cracker (Keebler) | 1 piece | 44 |
| Corn chips: | | |
| (Featherweight) low sodium | 1 oz. | 3 |
| (Flavor Tree) | 1 oz. | 260 |
| *Fritos:* | | |
| Regular | 1 oz. | 204 |
| Barbecue flavor | 1 oz. | 270 |
| *Korkers* (Nabisco) | 1 piece | 11 |
| (Laura Scudder's) | 1 oz. | 125 |
| (Tom's) regular | 1 oz. | 200 |
| *Crown Pilot* (Nabisco) | 1 piece | 64 |
| English Water Biscuit | | |
| (Pepperidge Farm) | 1 piece | 24 |
| *Escort* (Nabisco) | 1 piece | 37 |
| French onion cracker (Nabisco) | 1 piece | 31 |
| *Goldfish* (Pepperidge Farm): | | |
| Thins | 1 piece | 15 |
| Tiny | 1 piece | 5 |
| Graham: | | |
| (Dixie Belle) sugar-honey coated | 1 piece | 26 |
| Graham, chocolate or cocoa-covered: | | |
| *Fancy Dip* (Nabisco) | 1 piece | 41 |
| (Keebler) | 1 piece | 27 |
| (Nabisco) | 1 piece | 34 |
| Melba Toast (See MELBA TOAST) | | |
| Nachips (Old El Paso) | 1 piece | 11 |
| Nacho rings (Tom's) | 1 oz. | 330 |
| Oyster: | | |
| (Dixie Belle) | 1 piece | 11 |
| (Keebler) *Zesta* | 1 piece | 4 |
| (Nabisco) *Dandy* or *Oysterettes* | 1 piece | 11 |
| Party Mix (Flavor Tree): | | |
| Regular | 1 oz. | 400 |
| No salt added | 1 oz. | 10 |
| Rich & Crisp (Ralston) | 1 piece | 18 |
| *Ritz* (Nabisco) | 1 piece | 32 |
| *Roman Meal Wafer*, boxed | 1 piece | 20 |
| *Royal Lunch* (Nabisco) | 1 piece | 66 |

| Food and Description | Measure or Quantity | Sodium (mgs.) |
|---|---|---|
| *Ry-Krisp:* | | |
| Natural | 1 triple cracker | 48 |
| Seasoned | 1 triple cracker | 65 |
| Sesame | 1 triple cracker | 75 |
| Rye wafers (Nabisco) | 1 piece | 23 |
| Saltine: | | |
| (Dixie Belle) regular | 1 piece | 36 |
| *Flavor Kist* (Schulze and Burch) | 1 piece | 12 |
| *Premium* (Nabisco) | 1 piece | 35 |
| (Ralston) unsalted top | 1 piece | 21 |
| *Zesta* (Keebler) | 1 piece | 34 |
| Sea Toast (Keebler) | 1 piece | 112 |
| Sesame: | | |
| (Flavor Tree): | | |
| Crunch | 1 oz. | 70 |
| Stick: | | |
| Plain | 1 oz. | 405 |
| With bran | 1 oz. | 370 |
| No salt added | 1 oz. | 10 |
| (Nabisco) butter flavored | 1 piece | 35 |
| (Pepperidge Farm) | 1 piece | 28 |
| Snackers (Ralston) | 1 piece | 23 |
| *Snackin' Crisp* (Durkee) *O & C* | 1 oz. | 257 |
| Snacks Sticks (Pepperidge Farm): | | |
| Cheese or sesame | 1 piece | 17 |
| Lightly salted | 1 piece | 40 |
| Pumpernickel or rye | 1 piece | 48 |
| Sour cream & onion sticks (Flavor Tree) | 1 oz. | 415 |
| Taco chips (Laura Scudder's) mini | 1 oz. | 200 |
| Tortilla chips: | | |
| *Doritos,* nacho | 1 oz. | 108 |
| (Laura Scudder's) | 1 oz. | 90 |
| (Planters) nacho or taco | 1 oz. | 170 |
| (Tom's) | 1 oz. | 180 |
| *Town House Cracker* (Keebler) | 1 piece | 42 |
| *Triscuit* (Nabisco) | 1 piece | 30 |
| *Twigs* (Nabisco) | 1 piece | 32 |
| *Uneeda Biscuit* (Nabisco) unsalted | 1 piece | 35 |
| Unsalted (Featherweight) | 2 sections (½ cracker) | 1 |
| *Waldorf* (Keebler) low sodium | 1 piece | Tr. |
| *Waverly Wafer* (Nabisco) | 1 piece | 46 |
| Wheat (Pepperidge Farm) cracked | 1 piece | 52 |
| Wheat nuts (Flavor Tree) | 1 oz. | 185 |
| Wheat Snack (Dixie Belle) | 1 piece | 12 |
| *Wheat Thins* (Nabisco) | 1 piece | 23 |

46

| Food and Description | Measure or Quantity | Sodium (mgs.) |
|---|---|---|
| Wheat Toast (Keebler) | 1 piece | 25 |
| Wheatwafer (Estee) *6 Calorie* | 1 piece | <5 |
| Wheat wafer (Featherweight) | | |
| **CRACKER CRUMBS,** graham (Nabisco) | ⅛ of 9″ pie shell | 102 |
| **CRACKER MEAL** (Nabisco) salted | 1 cup | 1022 |
| *CRANAPPLE JUICE* | | |
| Canned (Ocean Spray): | | |
| Regular | 6 fl. oz. | 4 |
| Dietetic | 6 fl. oz. | 8 |
| **CRANBERRY,** fresh (Ocean Spray) | ½ cup | Tr. |
| ***CRANBERRY-GRAPE JUICE,*** | | |
| Canned (Ocean Spray) *Crangrape* | 6 fl. oz. | 5 |
| **CRANBERRY JUICE COCKTAIL** | | |
| Canned (Ocean Spray): | | |
| Regular | 6 fl. oz. | 3 |
| Dietetic | 6 fl. oz. | 6 |
| **CRANBERRY-ORANGE RELISH** (Ocean Spray) | 2 oz. | 18 |
| **CRANBERRY-RASPBERRY SAUCE** (Ocean Spray) jellied | 2 oz. | 14 |
| **CRANBERRY SAUCE:** | | |
| Home recipe | 4 oz. | 1 |
| Canned (Ocean Spray): | | |
| Jellied | 2 oz. | 17 |
| Whole berry | 2 oz. | 16 |
| *CRANTASTIC,* juice drink (Ocean Spray) | 6 fl. oz. | <10 |
| *CRAZY COW,* cereal (General Mills) | 1 cup | 185 |
| **CREAM:** | | |
| Half & Half | 1 T. | 7 |
| Light, table or coffee (Sealtest) 16% fat | 1 T. | 6 |
| Light, whipping, 30% fat (Sealtest) | 1 T. | 5 |
| Heavy whipping | ½ cup | 38 |
| Sour | 1 T. | 5 |
| Substitute (See CREAM SUBSTITUTE) | | |
| **CREAM PUFFS:** | | |
| Home recipe, custard filling | 3½″ × 2″ piece | 108 |
| Frozen (Rich's) chocolate | 1⅓-oz. piece | 83 |
| **CREAM SUBSTITUTE:** | | |
| *Coffee Mate* (Carnation) | 1 tsp. | 4 |
| *Coffee Rich* | ½ oz. | 7 |
| *N-Rich* | 1½ tsp. | 17 |
| **CREPE,** frozen: | | |
| (Mrs. Paul's): | | |
| Crab | 5½-oz. pkg. | 1156 |

| Food and Description | Measure or Quantity | Sodium (mgs.) |
|---|---|---|
| Shrimp | 5½-oz. pkg. | 1046 |
| (Stouffer's): | | |
| Chicken with mushroom sauce | 8¼-oz. pkg. | 390 |
| Ham & asparagus | 6¼-oz. pkg. | 804 |
| Spinach with cheddar | | |
| cheese sauce | 9½-oz. pkg. | 995 |
| **CRISP RICE CEREAL:** | | |
| (Featherweight) low sodium | 1 cup | 110 |
| (Ralston Purina) | 1 cup | 110 |
| ***CRISPY WHEATS'N RAISINS,*** | | |
| cereal (General Mills) | ¾ cup | 180 |
| **CROQUETTES,** frozen, seafood | | |
| (Mrs. Paul's) | 3-oz. serving | 869 |
| **CROUTON:** | | |
| (Arnold): | | |
| Bavarian or English style | ½ oz. | 65 |
| French, Italian or Mexican style | ½ oz. | 66 |
| (Kellogg's) *Croutettes* | ⅔ cup | 260 |
| (Pepperidge Farm): | | |
| Cheddar & romano or sour cream | | |
| & chive | .5 oz. | 185 |
| Cheese & garlic | .5 oz. | 175 |
| Onion & garlic | .5 oz. | 160 |
| Seasoned | .5 oz. | 215 |
| ***C-3PO's #,*** cereal (Kellogg's) | ¾ cup | 160 |
| **CUCUMBER:** | | |
| Eaten with skin | 8-oz. cucumber | 13 |
| Pared, 10-oz. cucumber | 7½" × 2" pared | 12 |
| Pared | 3 slices | Tr. |
| **CUMIN SEED** (French's) | 1 tsp. | 3 |
| **CUPCAKE:** | | |
| Regular (Hostess): | | |
| Chocolate | 1 cupcake | 250 |
| Orange | 1 cupcake | 175 |
| Frozen (Sara Lee) yellow | 1 cupcake | 161 |
| ***CUPCAKE MIX** (Flako) | 1 cupcake | 195 |
| **CURRANT, DRIED** (Del Monte) | | |
| Zante | ½ cup | 4 |
| **CURRANT JELLY** (Smucker's) | 1 T. | 7 |
| **CURRY POWDER** (Durkee) | 1 tsp. | 63 |
| **CUSTARD:** | | |
| Chilled, *Swiss Miss,* chocolate | 4-oz. container | 149 |
| *Mix, dietetic (Featherweight) | ½ cup | 105 |
| ***C.W. POST,*** cereal: | | |
| Plain | ¼ cup | 49 |
| With raisins | ¼ cup | 44 |

# D

| Food and Description | Measure or Quantity | Sodium (mgs.) |
|---|---|---|
| **DAIRY QUEEN/BRAZIER:** | | |
| Banana split | 13.5-oz. serving | 153 |
| *Brownie Delight*, hot fudge | 9.4-oz. serving | 227 |
| *Buster Bar* | 5¼-oz. piece | 179 |
| Chicken sandwich | 7.8-oz. sandwich | 869 |
| Cone: | | |
| Plain, any flavor: | | |
| Small | 3-oz. cone | 47 |
| Regular | 5-oz. cone | 18 |
| Large | 7½-oz. cone | 117 |
| Dipped, chocolate: | | |
| Small | 3¼-oz. cone | 55 |
| Regular | 5½-oz. cone | 94 |
| Large | 8¼-oz. cone | 140 |
| *Dilly Bar* | 3-oz. piece | 51 |
| *Double Delight* | 9-oz. serving | 153 |
| *DQ Sandwich* | 2.1-oz. sandwich | 39 |
| Fish sandwich: | | |
| Plain | 6-oz. sandwich | 875 |
| With cheese | 6¼-oz. sandwich | 1035 |
| Float | 14-oz. serving | 79 |
| Freeze, vanilla | 14-oz. serving | 179 |
| French fries: | | |
| Regular | 2½-oz. serving | 114 |
| Large | 4-oz. serving | 181 |
| Frozen dessert | 4-oz. serving | 62 |
| Hamburger: | | |
| Plain: | | |
| Single | 5.2-oz. burger | 630 |
| Double | 7.4-oz. burger | 660 |
| Triple | 9.6-oz. burger | 690 |
| With cheese: | | |
| Single | 5.7-oz. burger | 790 |
| Double | 8.4-oz. burger | 980 |
| Triple | 10.62-oz. burger | 1010 |

| Food and Description | Measure or Quantity | Sodium (mgs.) |
|---|---|---|
| Hot dog: | | |
| Regular: | | |
| Plain | 3.5-oz. serving | 830 |
| With cheese | 4-oz. serving | 990 |
| With chili | 4½-oz. serving | 985 |
| Super: | | |
| Plain | 6.2-oz. serving | 1365 |
| With cheese | 6.9-oz. serving | 1605 |
| With chili | 7.7-oz. serving | 1595 |
| Lettuce | ½ oz. | <10 |
| Malt, chocolate: | | |
| Small | 10¼-oz. serving | 180 |
| Regular | 14¾-oz. serving | 260 |
| Large | 20¾-oz. serving | 360 |
| *Mr. Misty:* | | |
| Plain: | | |
| Small | 8¼-oz. serving | <10 |
| Regular | 11.64-oz. serving | <10 |
| Large | 15½-oz. serving | <10 |
| *Kiss* | 3.14-oz. serving | <10 |
| Float | 14.5-oz. serving | 95 |
| Freeze | 14.5-oz. serving | 140 |
| Onion rings | 3-oz. serving | 140 |
| Parfait | 10-oz. serving | 140 |
| *Peanut Butter Parfait* | 10¾-oz. serving | 250 |
| Shake, chocolate: | | |
| Small | 10¼-oz. serving | 180 |
| Regular | 14¾-oz. serving | 260 |
| Large | 20¾-oz. serving | 360 |
| Strawberry shortcake | 11-oz. serving | 215 |
| Sundae, chocolate: | | |
| Small | 3¾-oz. serving | 75 |
| Regular | 6¼-oz. serving | 120 |
| Large | 8¾-oz. serving | 165 |
| Tomato | ½ oz. | <10 |
| **DAIQUIRI COCKTAIL** | | |
| (Mr. Boston): | | |
| Regular | 3 fl. oz. | 51 |
| Strawberry | 3 fl. oz. | 64 |
| **DATE:** | | |
| Chopped | ¼ cup | Tr. |
| Pitted, whole | 5 dates | Tr. |
| ***DELI'S,*** frozen (Pepperidge Farm): | | |
| Beef with barbecue sauce | 4-oz. piece | 685 |
| Mexican style | 4-oz. piece | 645 |
| Reuben in rye pastry | 4-oz. piece | 650 |
| Savory chicken salad | 4-oz. piece | 625 |

| Food and Description | Measure or Quantity | Sodium (mgs.) |
|---|---|---|
| Turkey, ham & cheese | 4-oz. piece | 740 |
| Western style omelet | 4-oz. piece | 555 |
| **DESSERT CUPS** (Hostess) | ¾-oz. piece | 120 |
| **DILL SEED** (French's) | 1 tsp. | Tr. |
| **DING DONG** (Hostess) | 1 cake | 130 |
| **DINNER, FROZEN** (See individual listings such as BEEF, CHICKEN, TURKEY, etc.) | | |
| **DIP:** | | |
| Blue cheese (Dean) | 1 oz. | 14 |
| Enchilada, *Fritos* | 1 oz. | 97 |
| Jalapeno, *Fritos* | 1 oz. | 88 |
| Onion (Dean) French | 1 oz. | 20 |
| **DISTILLED LIQUOR,** any brand, any proof | 1 fl. oz. | Tr. |
| **DONUTZ,** cereal (General Mills): | | |
| Chocolate | 1 cup | 210 |
| Powdered | 1 cup | 185 |
| **DOUGHNUT:** | | |
| Regular (Hostess): | | |
| Chocolate coated | 1-oz. piece | 150 |
| Cinnamon | 1-oz. piece | 140 |
| *Donettes,* powdered | 1 piece | 40 |
| Old fashioned, plain | 1.5-oz. piece | 220 |
| Powdered | 1-oz. piece | 140 |
| Frozen (Morton): | | |
| Regular: | | |
| Bavarian creme | 2-oz. piece | 75 |
| Boston creme | 2.3-oz. piece | 90 |
| Chocolate iced | 1.5-oz. piece | 75 |
| Jelly | 1.8-oz. piece | 75 |
| *Donut Holes:* | | |
| Devil's Food | ⅕ of 7¾-oz. pkg. | 105 |
| Vanilla | ⅕ of 7¾-oz. pkg. | 123 |
| **DRUMSTICK,** frozen: | | |
| Ice Cream, in a cone: | | |
| Topped with peanuts | 1 piece | 82 |
| Topped with peanuts & cone bisque | 1 piece | 72 |
| Ice Milk, in a cone: | | |
| Topped with peanuts | 1 piece | 87 |
| Topped with peanuts & cone bisque | 1 piece | 77 |
| **DULCITA,** frozen (Hormel) apple | 4 oz. | 350 |
| **DUMPLINGS,** canned, dietetic (Dia-Mel) | 8-oz. serving | 70 |

# E

| Food and Description | Measure or Quantity | Sodium (mgs.) |
|---|---|---|
| **ECLAIR:** | | |
| Home recipe, with custard filling and chocolate icing | 4-oz. piece | 93 |
| Frozen (Rich's) chocolate | 1 piece | 194 |
| **EGG, CHICKEN:** | | |
| Raw: | | |
| White only | 1 large egg | 48 |
| Yolk only | 1 large egg | 9 |
| Boiled, without salt | 1 large egg | 61 |
| Fried in butter | 1 large egg | 155 |
| Omelet, mixed with milk & cooked in fat | 1 large egg | 159 |
| Poached | 1 large egg | 130 |
| Scrambled, mixed with milk & cooked in fat | 1 large egg | 164 |
| **EGG DINNER OR ENTREE,** frozen (Swanson): | | |
| Omelet, Spanish style | 8-oz. meal | 898 |
| Scrambled, with sausage | 6¼-oz. meal | 790 |
| **EGG MIX** (Durkee): | | |
| Omelet: | | |
| *With bacon | ½ pkg. | 276 |
| *Puffy | ½ pkg. | 333 |
| Scrambled: | | |
| Plain | .8-oz. pkg. | 320 |
| With bacon | 1.3-oz. pkg. | 476 |
| **EGG NOG COCKTAIL** (Mr. Boston) 15% alcohol | 3 fl. oz. | 71 |
| **EGGPLANT:** | | |
| Boiled, without salt | 4 oz. | 1 |
| Frozen: | | |
| (Mrs. Paul's): | | |
| Parmesan | 5½-oz. serving | 905 |
| Sticks, breaded & fried | 3½-oz. serving | 610 |
| (Weight Watchers) parmesan | 13-oz. pkg. | 285 |

| Food and Description | Measure or Quantity | Sodium (mgs.) |
|---|---|---|
| **EGG ROLL**, frozen (La Choy): | | |
| Chicken | .4-oz. roll | 62 |
| Lobster | .4-oz. roll | 80 |
| Meat & shrimp | .2-oz. roll | 42 |
| Meat & shrimp | .4-oz. roll | 73 |
| Shrimp | 3-oz. roll | 575 |
| **EGG SUBSTITUTE:** | | |
| *Egg Magic* (Featherweight) | ½ envelope | 123 |
| *Scramblers* (Morningstar Farms) | 1 egg substitute | 75 |
| *Second Nature* (Avoset) | 3 T. | 68 |
| **ELDERBERRY JELLY** (Smucker's) | 1 T. | Tr. |
| **ENCHILADA**, frozen: | | |
| Beef: | | |
| (Banquet): | | |
| *Buffet Supper* | 2-lb. pkg. | 5908 |
| Dinner | 12-oz. dinner | 1905 |
| (Green Giant) Sonora style | 12-oz. entree | 1245 |
| (Hormel) | 1 enchiladas | 573 |
| (Morton) | 11-oz. dinner | 1216 |
| (Swanson) *TV Brand* | 15-oz. dinner | 1575 |
| (Van de Kamp's): | | |
| Dinner | 12-oz. dinner | 2177 |
| Entree, shredded | 5½-oz. serving | 520 |
| Cheese: | | |
| (Banquet) Extra Helping | 21 ¼-oz. dinner | 4778 |
| (Hormel) | 1 enchilada | 676 |
| (Van de Kamp's) | 12-oz. dinner | 1664 |
| Chicken (Van de Kamp's) regular | 7½-oz. pkg. | 1108 |
| **ENCHILADA SAUCE:** | | |
| Canned: | | |
| (Del Monte) hot | ½ cup | 1151 |
| *Old El Paso*, hot or mild | ¼ cup | 248 |
| *Mix (Durkee) | ½ cup | 96 |
| **ENDIVE, CURLY OR ESCAROLE,** cut | ½ cup | 5 |

# F

| Food and Description | Measure or Quantity | Sodium (mgs.) |
|---|---|---|
| **FARINA:** | | |
| (Hi-O) dry, regular | ¼ cup | 2 |
| *Malt-O-Meal,* dry: | | |
| Regular | 1 oz. | 3 |
| Quick cooking | 1 oz. | 2 |
| *(Pillsbury) made with water and salt | ⅔ cup | 265 |
| **FAT, COOKING** | Any quantity | 0 |
| **FENNEL SEED** (French's) | 1 tsp. | 2 |
| **FETTUCINI ALFREDO,** frozen (Stouffer's) | 5-oz. serving | 1195 |
| **FIG:** | | |
| Small | 1½" fig | Tr. |
| Canned, regular pack (Del Monte) | | |
| whole, solids & liq. | ½ cup | <10 |
| Dried, chopped | ½ cup | 29 |
| **FIG JUICE,** (Sunsweet) | 6 fl. oz. | 24 |
| *FIGURINES* (Pillsbury): | | |
| Caramel nut | 1 bar | 143 |
| Chocolate | 1 bar | 115 |
| Chocolate caramel & lemon yogurt | 1 bar | 90 |
| Double chocolate | 1 bar | 130 |
| Strawberry yogurt | 1 bar | 83 |
| Vanilla | 1 bar | 90 |
| **FILBERT:** | | |
| Shelled | 1 oz. | Tr. |
| (Fisher) oil dipped, salted | ½ cup | 114 |
| **FISH CAKE,** frozen (Mrs. Paul's): | | |
| Breaded & fried, Beach Haven | 2-oz. piece | 405 |
| Thins, breaded & fried | ½ of 10-oz. pkg. | 1020 |
| **FISH & CHIPS,** frozen: | | |
| (Banquet) *Man-Pleaser* | 14-oz. dinner | 972 |
| (Swanson): | | |
| Regular | 5½-oz. entree | 585 |
| *Hungry Man* | 14¾-oz. dinner | 1280 |

| Food and Description | Measure or Quantity | Sodium (mgs.) |
|---|---|---|
| (Van de Kamp's) batter dipped, french fried | 8-oz. pkg. | 557 |
| **FISH DINNER,** frozen: | | |
| (Banquet) | 8¾-oz. dinner | 928 |
| (Morton) | 9-oz. dinner | 690 |
| (Mrs. Paul's): | | |
| Regular, parmesan | 5-oz. meal | 540 |
| Light: | | |
| Dijon | 8½-oz. meal | 925 |
| Mornay | 10-oz. meal | 665 |
| (Stouffer's) *Lean Cuisine,* florentine | 9-oz. meal | 815 |
| (Van de Kamp's) regular, french fried | 12-oz. dinner | 1822 |
| (Weight Watchers): | | |
| Au gratin | 9¼-oz. meal | 837 |
| Oven fried | 9-oz. meal | 542 |
| **FISH FILLET,** frozen: | | |
| (Mrs. Paul's): | | |
| Batter fried, crunchy | 2¼-oz. piece | 428 |
| Breaded & fried, crispy, crunchy | 2.1-oz. piece | 325 |
| Buttered | 2.5-oz. piece | 390 |
| (Van de Kamp's): | | |
| Batter dipped, french fried | 3-oz. piece | 352 |
| Country seasoned | 2.4-oz. piece | 334 |
| *Today's Catch* | 4-oz. serving | 130 |
| **FISH KABOBS,** frozen: | | |
| (Mrs. Paul's) light batter | ⅓ pkg. | 429 |
| (Van de Kamp's) batter dipped french fried | .4-oz. piece | 26 |
| **FISH SEASONING** (Featherweight) | ¼ tsp. | Tr. |
| **FISH STICKS,** frozen: | | |
| (Mrs. Paul's): | | |
| Batter fried | 1 piece | 199 |
| Breaded & fried, crispy | 1 piece | 114 |
| (Van de Kamp's) batter dipped, french fried | 1-oz. piece | 196 |
| ***FIT'N FROSTY*** (Alba '77): | | |
| Chocolate | 1 envelope | 93 |
| Strawberry | 1 envelope | 115 |
| Vanilla | 1 envelope | 108 |
| ***FIVE ALIVE*** (Snow Crop) | 6 fl. oz. | 1 |
| **FLOUNDER:** | | |
| Baked | 4 oz. | 269 |
| Frozen: | | |
| (Mrs. Paul's) fillets, breaded & fried, light & natural | 3-oz. piece | 487 |
| (Van de Kamp's) *Today's Catch* | 4-oz. serving | 220 |

| Food and Description | Measure or Quantity | Sodium (mgs.) |
|---|---|---|
| **FLOUR:** | | |
| (Aunt Jemima) self-rising | ¼ cup | 368 |
| *Ballard,* self-rising | ¼ cup | 323 |
| *Bisquick* (Betty Crocker) | ¼ cup | 350 |
| Chestnut | 1 oz. | 3 |
| (Elam's): | | |
|   Brown rice, whole grain | ¼ cup | 2 |
|   Buckwheat, pure | ¼ cup | 2 |
|   Pastry, whole wheat | ¼ cup | 2 |
|   Rye, whole grain | ¼ cup | 3 |
|   Soy, roasted | ¼ cup | 5 |
| *Gold Medal* (Betty Crocker) | | |
|   all-purpose or high protein | ¼ cup | 1 |
| *La Pina* | ¼ cup | 1 |
| *Pillsbury's Best:* | | |
|   All-purpose or rye, medium | ¼ cup | <2 |
|   Sauce & gravy | 2 T. | <3 |
|   Self-rising | ¼ cup | 392 |
| *Presto,* self-rising | ¼ cup | 322 |
| (Robin Hood) | ¼ cup | 0 |
| *Wondra* | ¼ cup | <3 |
| **FOOD STICKS** (Pillsbury) chocolate | 1 piece | 29 |
| **FRANKEN\*BERRY,** cereal | | |
| (General Mills) | 1 cup | 205 |
| **FRANKFURTER:** | | |
| (Eckrich): | | |
|   Beef or meat | 1.6-oz. frankfurter | 480 |
|   Beef or meat, jumbo | 2-oz. frankfurter | 620 |
|   Meat | 1.2-oz. frankfurter | 360 |
| (Hormel): | | |
|   Beef | 1.6-oz. frankfurter | 463 |
|   Chili, *Frank'n Stuff* | 1 frankfurter | 517 |
|   Meat | 1 frankfurter (12-oz. pkg.) | 378 |
| (Oscar Mayer): | | |
|   Beef | 1.6-oz. frankfurter | 466 |
|   Little Wiener | 2″ frankfurter | 103 |
|   Wiener | 1.6-oz. frankfurter | 514 |
|   Wiener, with cheese | 1.6-oz. frankfurter | 510 |
| *Wranglers* (Hormel) smoked: | | |
|   Beef | 1 frankfurter | 619 |
|   With cheese | 1 frankfurter | 546 |
| **FRENCH TOAST,** frozen: | | |
| (Aunt Jemima): | | |
|   Regular | 1 slice | 216 |
|   Cinnamon swirl | 1 slice | 179 |
| (Swanson) with sausage, | 6½-oz. pkg. | 820 |

| Food and Description | Measure or Quantity | Sodium (mgs.) |
|---|---|---|
| **FRITTERS, FROZEN** (Mrs. Paul's): | | |
| Apple | 2-oz. piece | 385 |
| Corn | 2-oz. piece | 363 |
| *FROOT-LOOPS*, cereal (Kellogg's) | 1 cup | 135 |
| **FROZEN DESERT**, dietetic (Baskin-Robbins) *Special Diet:*. | | |
| Mountain Coffee | 1 scoop (2½ fl. oz.) | 60 |
| Sunny orange | 1 scoop (2½ fl. oz.) | 60 |
| Wild strawberry | 1 scoop (2½ fl. oz.) | 60 |
| **FRUIT BITS,** dried (Sun-Maid) | 1 oz. | 24 |
| **FRUIT COCKTAIL:** | | |
| Canned, regular pack, solids & liq.: | | |
| (Del Monte) regular or chunky | ½ cup | <10 |
| (Libby's) | ½ cup | 8 |
| (Stokely-Van Camp) | ½ cup | 15 |
| Canned, dietetic or low calorie, solids & liq.: | | |
| (Del Monte) Lite | ½ cup | <10 |
| (Diet Delight) juice or water pack | ½ cup | <5 |
| (Featherweight) juice or water pack | ½ cup | <10 |
| (Libby's) water pack | ½ cup | 10 |
| **FRUIT CUP** (Del Monte): | | |
| Mixed fruits | 5-oz. container | 6 |
| Peaches, diced | 5-oz. container | 9 |
| *FRUIT & FIBER CEREAL* (Post): | | |
| With apple & cinnamon | ½ cup | 195 |
| With dates, raisins and walnuts | ½ cup | 170 |
| **FRUIT & JUICE BAR** (Dole): | | |
| Orange or strawberry | 2½-oz. bar | 6 |
| Pineapple | 2½-oz. bar | 4 |
| **FRUIT, MIXED:** | | |
| Canned (Del Monte) Lite, chunky, | ½ cup | <10 |
| Dried (Del Monte) | 2-oz. | 10 |
| Frozen (Birds Eye) quick thaw | 5-oz. serving | 4 |
| **FRUIT & NUT MIX** (Carnation) | .9-oz. pouch | 10 |
| **FRUIT PUNCH:** | | |
| Canned: | | |
| *Capri Sun* | 6¾ fl. oz. | 1 |
| (Hi-C) | 6 fl. oz. | Tr. |
| Chilled: | | |
| *Five Alive* (Snow Crop) | 6 fl. oz. | 1 |
| (Minute Maid) | 6 fl. oz. | Tr. |
| *Frozen, Five Alice* (Snow Crop) | 6 fl. oz. | 1 |

| Food and Description | Measure or Quantity | Sodium (mgs.) |
|---|---|---|
| *Mix, regular (Hi-C) | 6 fl. oz. | 1 |
| *Mix, dietetic, *Crystal Light* | 6 fl. oz. | Tr. |
| **FRUIT ROLLS:** | | |
| (Betty Crocker) | 1 piece | 5 |
| (Flavor Tree) | 1 piece | 15 |
| (Sunkist) | 1 piece | 10 |
| **FRUIT SALAD:** | | |
| Canned, regular pack: | | |
| (Del Monte) fruits for salad | ½ cup | <10 |
| (Libby's) | ½ cup | 8 |
| Canned, dietetic or low calorie | | |
| (Diet Delight) juice pack | ½ cup | 5 |
| ***FRUIT SQUARES,*** frozen | | |
| (Pepperidge Farm): | | |
| Apple | 2½-oz. piece | 175 |
| Blueberry | 2½-oz. piece | 190 |
| ***FUDGE JUMBLES*** (Pillsbury): | | |
| Brown sugar oatmeal | 1 bar | 60 |
| Peanut butter oatmeal | 1 bar | 55 |

# G

| Food and Description | Measure or Quantity | Sodium (mgs.) |
|---|---|---|
| **GARLIC:** | | |
| Whole | 2 oz. | 10 |
| Flakes (Gilroy) | 1 tsp. | Tr. |
| Powder (French's) | 1 tsp. | Tr. |
| Salt (French's) | 1 tsp. | 1850 |
| **GELFILTE FISH,** canned, jelled | | |
| (Rokeach) | 4-oz. serving | 835 |
| **GELATIN DESSERT, CANNED** | | |
| (Dia-Mel) *Gel-A-Thin* | 4-oz. serving | 5 |
| **\*GELATIN DESSERT MIX:** | | |
| Regular: | | |
| (Jell-O): | | |
| Apricot, black cherry or orange | ½ cup | 55 |
| Lemon | ½ cup | 81 |
| (Royal) all flavors | ½ cup | 91 |
| Dietetic: | | |
| *Carmel Kosher* | ½ cup | <10 |
| (Dia-Mel) *Gel-A-Thin* | ½ cup | 10 |
| (D-Zerta) all flavors | ½ cup | 5 |
| (Estee) all flavors | ½ cup | 10 |
| (Featherweight) artificially sweetened | ½ cup | 2 |
| (Jell-O): | | |
| Cherry | ½ cup | 80 |
| Raspberry or strawberry | ½ cup | 56 |
| **GELATIN, DRINKING** (Knox) orange | 1 envelope | 20 |
| **GERMAN STYLE DINNER,** frozen (Swanson) *TV Brand* | 11¾-oz. dinner | 668 |
| **GINGER,** powder (French's) | 1 tsp. | Tr. |
| **\*GINGERBREAD MIX:** | | |
| (Betty Crocker) | ⅑ pkg. | 325 |
| (Pillsbury) | 3" square | 310 |
| ***GOLDEN GRAHAMS,*** cereal (General Mills) | ¾ cup | 285 |

| Food and Description | Measure or Quantity | Sodium (mgs.) |
|---|---|---|
| **GOOSE,** roasted, meat | 4 oz. | 141 |
| **GRAHAM CRACKOS,** cereal (Kellogg's) | 1 cup | 145 |
| **GRANOLA BARS,** *Nature Valley:* | | |
| Regular: | | |
| Almond or peanut | 1 bar | 80 |
| Cinnamon or coconut | 1 bar | 65 |
| Peanut butter | 1 bar | 90 |
| Chewey: | | |
| Apple or raisin | 1 bar | 65 |
| Chocolate chip | 1 bar | 85 |
| **\*GRANOLA BAR MIX,** chewy, *Nature Valley, Bake-A-Bar,* chocolate chip | 1 bar | 40 |
| **GRANOLA CEREAL** *Nature Valley* | ⅓ cup | 35 |
| **GRANOLA CLUSTERS,** *Nature Valley:* | | |
| Almond | 1 piece | 140 |
| Apple-cinnamon | 1 piece | 125 |
| Caramel | 1 piece | 95 |
| **GRANOLA & FRUIT BAR,** *Nature Valley,* apple or raspberry | 1 bar | 150 |
| **GRANOLA SNACK,** *Nature Valley:* | | |
| Cinnamon or peanut butter | 1 pouch | 175 |
| Oats 'n Honey | 1 pouch | 170 |
| **GRAPE:** | | |
| American, ripe (slipskin) | 3½" × 3" bunch | 2 |
| Canned, dietetic (Featherweight) light, seedless, water pack | ½ cup | <10 |
| **GRAPE DRINK:** | | |
| Canned: | | |
| *Capri Sun* | 6¾ fl. oz. | 19 |
| (Hi-C) | 6 fl. oz. | Tr. |
| Mix: | | |
| Regular (Hi-C) | 6 fl. oz. | 42 |
| Dietetic (Sunkist) | 6 fl. oz. | 19 |
| **GRAPEFRUIT:** | | |
| Pink & red: | | |
| Seeded type | ½ med. grapefruit | 1 |
| Seedless type | ½ med. grapefruit | 1 |
| White: | | |
| Seeded type | ½ med. grapefruit | 1 |
| Seedless type | ½ med. grapefruit | 1 |
| Canned, regular pack (Del Monte) in syrup | ½ cup | 2 |
| Canned, dietetic pack, solids & liq.: | | |
| (Del Monte) sections | ½ cup | 2 |

| Food and Description | Measure or Quantity | Sodium (mgs.) |
|---|---|---|
| (Diet Delight) sections | ½ cup | 5 |
| (Featherweight) sections, juice pack | ½ cup | <10 |
| (S&W) *Nutradiet* | ½ cup | 40 |
| **GRAPEFRUIT JUICE:** | | |
| Fresh, pink, red or white | ½ cup | 1 |
| Canned, sweetened: | | |
| (Del Monte) | 6 fl. oz. | 2 |
| (Texsun) | 6 fl. oz. | 2 |
| Canned, unsweetened: | | |
| (Del Monte) | 6 fl. oz. | <10 |
| (Libby's) | 6 fl. oz. | 5 |
| (Ocean Spray) | 6 fl. oz. | 7 |
| (Texsun) | 6 fl. oz. | 2 |
| Chilled (Minute Maid) | 6 fl. oz. | 2 |
| *Frozen (Minute Maid) | 6 fl. oz. | 1 |
| **GRAPEFRUIT JUICE COCKTAIL,** | | |
| canned (Ocean Spray) pink | 6 fl. oz. | 15 |
| **GRAPE JELLY:** | | |
| Sweetened (Smucker's) | 1 T. | 6 |
| Dietetic: | | |
| (Dia-Mel) | 1 T. | <3 |
| (Featherweight) calorie reduced | 1 T. | 40-50 |
| (Louis Sherry) | 1 T. | <3 |
| **GRAPE JUICE:** | | |
| Canned, unsweetened | | |
| (Seneca Foods) | 6 fl. oz. | 4 |
| *Frozen (Minute Maid) | 6 fl. oz. | 2 |
| ***GRAPE NUTS,*** cereal (Post): | | |
| Regular | ¼ cup | 197 |
| Flakes | ⅞ cup | 218 |
| Raisin | ¼ cup | 160 |
| **GRAVY, CANNED:** | | |
| Au jus (Franco-American) | 2-oz. serving | 290 |
| Beef (Franco-American) | 2-oz. serving | 315 |
| Brown: | | |
| (Franco-American) with onion | 2-oz. serving | 340 |
| *Ready Gravy* | ¼ cup | <1 |
| Chicken: | | |
| (Franco-American) regular or giblet | 2-oz. serving | 320 |
| Mushroom (Franco-American) | 2-oz. serving | 320 |
| Pork (Franco-American) | 2 oz. | 350 |
| Turkey (Franco-American | 2-oz. serving | 300 |
| **GRAVYMASTER** | 1 tsp. | Tr. |
| **GRAVY WITH MEAT OR TURKEY:** | | |
| Canned (Morton House) sliced turkey | 6¼-oz. serving | 1076 |

| Food and Description | Measure or Quantity | Sodium (mgs.) |
|---|---|---|
| Frozen: | | |
| (Banquet): | | |
| Giblet gravy & sliced turkey, *Cookin' Bag* | 4-oz. pkg. | 492 |
| Sliced beef, *Buffet Supper* | 2-lb. pkg. | 3456 |
| (Morton) Family Meal: | | |
| Gravy & sliced beef | 2-lb. pkg. | 3000 |
| Gravy & turkey sliced | 2-lb. pkg. | 4480 |
| (Swanson) sliced beef | 8-oz. entree | 805 |
| **GRAVY MIX:** | | |
| Regular: | | |
| Au jus: | | |
| *(Durkee) | ½ cup | 456 |
| *(French's) *Gravy Makins* | ½ cup | 132 |
| Brown: | | |
| *(Durkee): | | |
| Regular | ½ cup | 518 |
| With mushrooms | ½ cup | 701 |
| *(French's) *Gravy Makins* | ½ cup | 180 |
| *(Pillsbury) | ½ cup | 305 |
| *(Spatini) | 2 oz. | 410 |
| Chicken: | | |
| (Durkee): | | |
| *Regular | ½ cup | 855 |
| *Roastin' Bag* | 1½-oz. pkg. | 3597 |
| *(French's) *Gravy Makins* | ½ cup | 300 |
| *(Pillsbury) | ½ cup | 230 |
| Home style: | | |
| *(Durkee) | ½ cup | 415 |
| *(French's) *Gravy Makins* | ½ cup | 670 |
| *(Pillsbury) | ½ cup | 600 |
| Meatloaf (Durkee) *Roastin Bag* | 1.5-oz. pkg. | 3472 |
| Mushroom: | | |
| *(Durkee) | ½ cup | 585 |
| *(French's) *Gravy Makins* | ½ cup | 610 |
| Onion: | | |
| *(Durkee) | ½ cup | 476 |
| *(French's) *Gravy Makins* | ½ cup | 700 |
| Pork: | | |
| *(Durkee) | ½ cup | 1087 |
| *(French's) *Gravy Makins* | ½ cup | 560 |
| *Swiss steak (Durkee) | ½ cup | 740 |
| Turkey: | | |
| *(Durkee) | ½ cup | 663 |
| *(French's) *Gravy Makins* | ½ cup | 760 |
| *Dietetic (Weight Watchers): | | |
| Brown | 1 pkg. | 1339 |

| Food and Description | Measure or Quantity | Sodium (mgs.) |
|---|---|---|
| Brown, with mushroom | 1 pkg. | 1495 |
| Brown, with onion | 1 pkg. | 1479 |
| Chicken | 1 pkg. | 2087 |
| **GREAT BEGINNINGS** (Hormel): | | |
| With chunky beef | 5 oz. | 904 |
| With turkey | 5 oz. | 585 |
| **GREENS, MIXED,** canned | | |
| (Sunshine) solids & liq. | ½ cup | 468 |
| **GUAVA,** flesh only | 1 guava | 3 |
| **GUAVA NECTAR** (Libby's) | 6 fl. oz. | 5 |

# H

| Food and Description | Measure or Quantity | Sodium (mgs.) |
|---|---|---|
| **HADDOCK:** | | |
| Fried, breaded | 4″ × 3″ × ½″ fillet | 176 |
| Frozen: | | |
| (Banquet) | 8¾-oz. dinner | 1770 |
| (Mrs. Paul's) breaded & fried light & natural | 2¼-oz. fillet | 468 |
| (Van de Kamp's) batter dipped, french fried | 2-oz. piece | 265 |
| **HALIBUT:** | | |
| Broiled | 4″ × 3″ × ½″ steak | 168 |
| Frozen (Van de Kamp's) batter dipped, french fried | ½ of 8-oz. pkg. | 618 |
| **HAM:** | | |
| Canned: | | |
| (Hormel): | | |
| *Black Label* | 4 oz. (3-lb. ham) | 1315 |
| Chunk | 6¾-oz. serving | 2241 |
| Chopped | 3 oz. | 1062 |
| Patties | 1 patty | 456 |
| (Oscar Mayer) *Jubilee*, extra lean, cooked | 1-oz. serving | 346 |
| Deviled: | | |
| (Hormel) | 1 T. | 108 |
| (Underwood) | 1 T. | 142 |
| Packaged: | | |
| (Eckrich) cooked, sliced | 1.2-oz. slice | 470 |
| (Hormel) chopped | 1 slice | 347 |
| (Oscar Mayer): | | |
| Chopped | 1-oz. slice | 378 |
| Cooked, smoked | 1-oz. slice | 382 |
| *Jubilee*, boneless: | | |
| Sliced | 8-oz. slice | 3029 |
| Steak, 95% fat free | 2-oz. steak | 739 |
| **HAMBURGER** (See *McDONALD'S, BURGER KING, DAIRY QUEEN*, etc.) | | |

| Food and Description | Measure or Quantity | Sodium (mgs.) |
|---|---|---|
| **\*HAMBURGER MIX** *Hamburger Helper* (General Mills): | | |
| Beef noodle | ⅕ pkg. | 970 |
| Cheeseburger macaroni | ⅕ pkg. | 1025 |
| Hash | ⅕ pkg. | 920 |
| Lasagna | ⅕ pkg. | 1000 |
| Pizza dish | ⅕ pkg. | 960 |
| Potatoes au gratin | ⅕ pkg. | 890 |
| Rice Oriental | ⅕ pkg. | 1085 |
| Stew | ⅕ pkg. | 945 |
| Tamale pie | ⅕ pkg. | 910 |
| **HAMBURGER SEASONING MIX:** | | |
| \*(Durkee) | 1 cup | 1012 |
| (French's) | 1-oz. pkg. | 1800 |
| **HAM AND CHEESE:** | | |
| (Eckrich) packaged | 1-oz. | 350 |
| (Hormel) patty, canned | 1 patty | 468 |
| (Oscar Mayer) loaf | 1-oz. serving | 370 |
| **HAM DINNER,** frozen: | | |
| (Banquet) American Favorites | 10-oz. dinner | 1148 |
| (Morton) | 10-oz. dinner | 375 |
| (Swanson) *TV Brand* | 10¼-oz. dinner | 1250 |
| **HAM SALAD,** canned (Carnation) | ¼ of 7½-oz. can | 84 |
| **HAM SALAD SPREAD** | | |
| (Oscar Mayer) | 1 oz. | 259 |
| **HEADCHEESE** (Oscar Mayer) | 1-oz. serving | 357 |
| **HERRING, SMOKED,** hard | 4-oz. serving | 7066 |
| **HO-HO** (Hostess) | 1-oz. piece | 90 |
| **HOMINY GRITS:** | | |
| Dry: | | |
| (Aunt Jemima) | 3 T. | <3 |
| (Quaker): | | |
| Regular | 3 T. | 101 |
| Instant: | | |
| Regular or quick | .8-oz. packet | <3 |
| With imitation bacon | 1-oz. packet | 544 |
| Cooked | 1 cup | 502 |
| **HONEY,** strained | 1 T. | 1 |
| **HONEYCOMB,** cereal (Post) regular | 1 ⅓ cups | 214 |
| **HONEYDEW** | 2″ × 7″ wedge | 11 |
| **HORSERADISH:** | | |
| Raw, pared | 1 oz. | 2 |
| Prepared | 1 oz. | 27 |
| **HOSTESS O'S** (Hostess) | 2¼-oz. piece | 265 |

# I

| Food and Description | Measure or Quantity | Sodium (mgs.) |
|---|---|---|
| **ICE CREAM** (See also FROZEN DESSERT): | | |
| *Bon-Bon*(Carnation): | | |
|   Chocolate | 1 piece | 11 |
|   Vanilla | 1 piece | 8 |
| Butter pecan: | | |
|   (Baskin Robbins) | 2½-fl.-oz. scoop | 81 |
|   (Häagen-Dazs) | 4 fl. oz. | 148 |
| Carob (Häagen-Dazs) | 4 fl. oz. | 101 |
| Cherry vanilla (Häagen-Dazs) | 4 fl. oz. | 68 |
| Chip crunch bar (Good Humor) | 3-fl.-oz.bar | 35 |
| Chocolate: | | |
|   (Baskin-Robbins): | | |
|     Regular | 2½-fl.-oz. scoop | 80 |
|     Mint | 2½-fl.-oz. scoop | 60 |
|     Mousse Royale | 2½-fl.-oz. scoop | 94 |
|   (Häagen Dazs) | 4 fl. oz. | 122 |
| Chocolate Eclair Bar (Good Humor) | 3-fl.-oz. bar | 70 |
| Chocolate fudge cake (Good Humor) | 3-fl.-oz. bar | 95 |
| Chocolate malt bar (Good Humor) | 3-fl.-oz.-bar | 50 |
| Coffee (Häagen-Dazs) | 4 fl. oz. | 135 |
| *Fat Frog* (Good Humor) | 3-fl.-oz. pop | 45 |
| *Heart* (Good Humor) | 4-fl.-oz. pop | 60 |
| Jamocha (Baskin-Robbins) | 2½-fl.-oz. scoop | 64 |
| Mocha chip (Häagen Dazs) | 4 fl. oz. | 68 |
| Peach (Häagen Dazs) | 4 fl. oz | 384 |
| Pralines'n Cream (Baskin-Robbins) | 2½-fl.-oz. scoop | 166 |
| Rocky Road (Baskin-Robbins) | 2½-fl.-oz. scoop | 77 |
| Rum raisin (Häagen Dazs) | 4 fl. oz. | 495 |
| Shark Bar (Good Humor) | 3-fl.-oz. pop | 0 |
| Strawberry: | | |
|   (Baskin-Robbins) | 2½-fl.-oz. scoop | 68 |
|   (Häagen Dazs) | 4 fl. oz. | 170 |
| Swiss chocolate almond (Häagen-Dazs) | 4 fl. oz. | 73 |
| Toasted almond bar (Good Humor) | 3-fl.-oz. pop | 30 |

| Food and Description | Measure or Quantity | Sodium (mgs.) |
|---|---|---|
| Vanilla: | | |
| (Baskin-Robbins) French | 2½-fl-oz. pop | 60 |
| (Häagen-Dazs) | 4 fl. oz. | 110 |
| Vanilla bar (Good Humor) chocolate coated | 3-fl.-oz. piece | 40 |
| Vanilla sandwich (Good Humor) | 2½-fl.-oz. piece | 120 |
| Vanilla slice (Good Humor) | 3.2-fl.-oz. piece | 45 |
| *Whammy* (Good Humor) | 1.6-oz. piece | 25 |
| **ICE CREAM CONE,** cone only | 1 piece | 12 |
| **\*ICE CREAM MIX** (Salada): | | |
| Dutch Chocolate | 1 cup | 75 |
| Peach, vanilla or wild strawberry | 1 cup | 60 |
| **ITALIAN DINNER,** frozen (Banquet) | 12-oz. dinner | 1783 |

# J

| Food and Description | Measure or Quantity | Sodium (mgs.) |
|---|---|---|
| **JELL-O FRUIT & CREAM BAR:** | | |
| Blueberry, raspberry or strawberry | 1.7-oz. piece | 98 |
| Peach | 1.7-oz. piece | 109 |
| **JELL-O GELATIN POPS** | 1.7-oz. piece | 7 |
| **JELLO PUDDING POPS:** | | |
| Banana, butterscotch or vanilla | 2-oz. piece | 63 |
| Chocolate or chocolate fudge | 2-oz. piece | 99 |
| Chocolate & vanilla swirl | 2-oz. piece | 81 |

# K

| Food and Description | Measure or Quantity | Sodium (mgs.) |
|---|---|---|
| **KABOOM,** cereal (General Mills) | 1 cup | 370 |
| **KALE:** | | |
| Boiled, without salt, leaves only | 4 oz. | 49 |
| Canned (Sunshine) chopped, solids & liq. | ½ cup | 251 |
| Frozen: | | |
| (Birds Eye) chopped | ⅓ pkg. | 14 |
| (McKenzie) chopped | 3⅓ oz. | 14 |
| **KARO SYRUP** (see SYRUP) | | |
| **KIDNEY:** | | |
| Beef, braised | 4 oz. | 287 |
| Lamb, raw | 4 oz. | 257 |
| **KIELBASA** (Hormel) Kolbase | 3-oz. serving | 1020 |
| **KING VITAMAN,** cereal (Quaker) | 1¼ cups | 251 |
| **KIX,** cereal | 1½ cups | 315 |
| ***KOOL-AID** (General Foods): | | |
| Unsweetened (sugar to be added): | | |
| Apple, grape or lemon-lime | 8 fl. oz. | Tr. |
| Strawberry | 8 fl. oz. | 33 |
| Tropical punch | 8 fl. oz. | 5 |
| Pre-sweetened with sugar: | | |
| Apple, grape, orange or raspberry | 8 fl. oz. | Tr. |
| Tropical punch | 8 fl. oz. | 10 |
| Pre-sweetened, dietetic, sugar free: | | |
| Cherry | 8 fl. oz. | 7 |
| Grape | 8 fl. oz. | Tr. |
| **KUMQUAT,** flesh & skin | 4 oz | 8 |

# L

| Food and Description | Measure or Quantity | Sodium (mgs.) |
|---|---|---|
| **LAMB:** | | |
| Leg: | | |
| Roasted, lean & fat | 4 oz. | 79 |
| Roasted, lean only | 4 oz. | 79 |
| Loin, one 5-oz. chop (weighed with bone before cooking) will give you: | | |
| Lean & fat | 2.8 oz. | 55 |
| Lean only | 2.3 oz. | 46 |
| Rib, one 5-oz. chop (weighed with bone before cooking) will give you: | | |
| Lean & fat | 2.9 oz. | 57 |
| Lean only | 2 oz. | 39 |
| Shoulder: | | |
| Roasted, lean & fat | 4 oz. | 79 |
| Roasted, lean only | 4 oz. | 79 |
| **LARD** | Any quantity | 0 |
| **LASAGNA:** | | |
| Canned (Hormel) *Short Orders* | 7½-oz. can | 1083 |
| Frozen: | | |
| (Green Giant): | | |
| Bake: | | |
| Regular, with meat sauce | 12-oz. entree | 1660 |
| Chicken | 12-oz. entree | 1215 |
| *Boil'N Bag* | 9½-oz. entree | 1145 |
| (Stouffer's): | | |
| Regular | 10½-oz. serving | 1200 |
| *Lean Cuisine*, zucchini | 11-oz. serving | 1000 |
| (Swanson): | | |
| Regular, 4-compartment dinner | 13-oz. dinner | 780 |
| *Hungry Man*, with meat | 18¾-oz. dinner | 1395 |
| Main Course, with meat | 13¼-oz. entree | 1160 |
| (Weight Watchers) regular | 12-oz. meal | 1345 |
| **LEEKS**, trimmed | 4 oz. | 6 |
| **LEMON:** | | |
| Whole | 2⅛" lemon | 3 |

| Food and Description | Measure or Quantity | Sodium (mgs.) |
|---|---|---|
| Peeled | 2⅛" lemon | 1 |
| **LEMONADE:** | | |
| Canned: | | |
| *Capri Sun* | 6¾ fl. oz. | 2 |
| *Country Time* | 6 fl. oz. | 46 |
| (Hi-C) | 6 fl. oz. | 6 |
| Chilled (Minute Maid) regular | | |
| or pink | 6 fl. oz. | Tr. |
| *Frozen: | | |
| *Country Time*, regular or pink | 6 fl. oz. | 11 |
| *Minute Maid* or (Sunkist) | 6 fl. oz. | Tr. |
| *Mix, regular: | | |
| *Country Time*, regular or pink | 6 fl. oz. | 12 |
| (Hi-C) | 6 fl. oz. | 6 |
| *Kool-Aid*, regular or pink | 6 fl. oz. | Tr. |
| *Mix, dietetic, *Crystal Light* | 6 fl. oz. | Tr. |
| **LEMONADE BAR** (Sunkist) | 3-fl.-oz. bar | 5 |
| **LEMON JUICE:** | | |
| Canned | 1 T. | Tr. |
| *Frozen (Minute Maid) | | |
| unsweetened | 1 fl. oz. | Tr. |
| ***LEMON-LIMEADE MIX** | | |
| (Minute Maid) | 6 fl. oz. | 6 |
| **LEMON-PEPPER SEASONING** | | |
| (French's) | 1 tsp. | 800 |
| **LENTIL,** whole, dry | 1 oz. | 9 |
| **LETTUCE:** | | |
| Bibb or Boston | 4" head | 15 |
| Cos or Romaine, shredded or | | |
| broken into pieces | ½ cup | 2 |
| Grand Rapids, Salad Bowl | | |
| or Simpson | 2 large leaves | 4 |
| Iceberg, New York or Great Lakes | ¼ of 4¾" head | 10 |
| *LIFE,* cereal (Quaker): | | |
| Regular | ⅔ cup | 163 |
| Cinnamon | ⅔ cup | 149 |
| *LIL' ANGELS* (Hostess) | 1-oz. piece | 95 |
| **LIME,** peeled | 2" dia. | 1 |
| ***LIMEADE,** frozen (Minute Maid) | 6 fl. oz. | Tr. |
| **LIME JUICE** | 1 T. | Tr. |
| **LIVER:** | | |
| Beef: | | |
| Fried | 6½" × 2⅜" × ⅜" slice | 156 |
| Cooked (Swift) | 3.2-oz. serving | 70 |

| Food and Description | Measure or Quantity | Sodium (mgs.) |
|---|---|---|
| Calf, fried | 6½" × 2⅛" × ⅜" slice | 100 |
| Chicken, simmered | 2" × 2" × ⅝" piece | 15 |
| **LIVERWURST SPREAD** | | |
| (Underwood) | ½ of 4¾-oz. can | 570 |
| **LOBSTER:** | | |
| Cooked, meat only | 1 cup | 304 |
| Canned, meat only | 4-oz. serving | 238 |
| **LOBSTER NEWBURG** | 1 cup | 572 |
| **LOBSTER SALAD,** home recipe | 4-oz. serving | 141 |
| **LONG ISLAND TEA COCKTAIL** | | |
| (Mr. Boston) | 3 fl. oz. | 34 |
| ***LONG JOHN SILVER'S:*** | | |
| Catfish fillet | 2.7-oz. piece | 469 |
| Catsup | .4 oz. | 136 |
| Chicken Plank | 1.4-oz. piece | 295 |
| Chicken Sandwich | 6.1-oz. sandwich | 1159 |
| Chowder, Clam | 1 order | 611 |
| Clams, breaded | 4.7-oz. order | 1170 |
| Cole Slaw | 3½ oz. (drained on fork) | 367 |
| Cracker | 1 piece | 36 |
| Fish Fillet: | | |
| Baked, with sauce | 5.5-oz. serving | 361 |
| Batter fried | 3-oz. piece | 673 |
| Kitchen breaded | 2-oz. piece | 374 |
| Fish sandwich | 6.4-oz. sandwich | 1243 |
| Fryer | 3-oz. serving | 6 |
| Hush Puppies | .85-oz. piece | 202 |
| Oyster, breaded, fried | .7-oz. piece | 65 |
| Peg Leg, battered | 1-oz. piece | 225 |
| Pie: | | |
| Apple | 4-oz. piece | 247 |
| Cherry | 4-oz. piece | 251 |
| Lemon meringue | 3½-oz. piece | 254 |
| Pecan | 4-oz. piece | 435 |
| Pumpkin | 4-oz. piece | 242 |
| Scallop, batter fried | .7-oz. piece | 201 |
| Seafood salad | 5.8 oz. serving | 833 |
| Seafood sauce | 1.2-oz. serving | 358 |
| Shrimp: | | |
| Batter fried | .6-oz. piece | 154 |
| Breaded, fried | 4.7-oz. order | 1229 |
| Chilled | .2-oz. piece | 19 |
| Vegetables, mixed | 4-oz. serving | 570 |
| ***LUCKY CHARMS,*** cereal | | |
| (General Mills) | 1 cup | 185 |

| Food and Description | Measure or Quantity | Sodium (mgs.) |
|---|---|---|
| **LUNCHEON MEAT** (See also individual listings such as BOLOGNA, HAM, etc.): | | |
| All meat (Oscar Mayer) | 1-oz. slice | 363 |
| Banquet loaf (Eckrich) | ¾-oz. slice | 250 |
| Bar-B-Que Loaf (Oscar Mayer) 90% fat free | 1-oz. slice | 374 |
| Beef, jellied (Hormel) loaf | 1 slice | 450 |
| Gourmet loaf (Eckrich) | 1-oz. slice | 390 |
| Ham & cheese (See HAM & CHEESE) | | |
| Ham roll sausage (Oscar Mayer) | 1-oz. slice | 329 |
| Honey loaf: | | |
| (Eckrich) regular | 1-oz. slice | 350 |
| (Hormel) | 1 slice | 292 |
| (Oscar Mayer) 95% fat free | 1-oz. slice | 378 |
| Iowa brand (Hormel) | 1 slice | 303 |
| Liver cheese (Oscar Mayer) | 1.3-oz. slice | 456 |
| Liver loaf (Hormel) | 1 slice | 352 |
| Luncheon roll sausage (Oscar Mayer) | 8-oz. slice | 222 |
| Luxury loaf (Oscar Mayer) 95% fat free | 1-oz. slice | 332 |
| Macaroni-cheese loaf (Eckrich) | 1-oz. slice | 370 |
| New England brand sliced sausage: | | |
| (Eckrich) | 1-oz. slice | 440 |
| (Hormel) | 1-oz. slice | 310 |
| (Oscar Mayer) 92% fat free | .8-oz. slice | 180 |
| Old fashioned loaf (Oscar Mayer) | 1-oz. slice | 344 |
| Olive loaf: | | |
| (Eckrich) | 1-oz. slice | 370 |
| (Hormel) | 1 slice | 405 |
| (Oscar Mayer) | 1-oz. slice | 406 |
| Peppered loaf: | | |
| (Eckrich) | 1-oz. slice | 390 |
| (Oscar Mayer) 93% fat free | 1-oz. slice | 405 |
| Pickle loaf: | | |
| (Eckrich) | 1-oz. slice | 320 |
| (Hormel) | 1-oz. slice | 376 |
| Pickle & pimiento (Oscar Mayer) | 1-oz. slice | 387 |
| Picnic loaf (Oscar Mayer) | 1-oz. slice | 325 |
| Spiced (Hormel) | 1 slice | 351 |

# M

| Food and Description | Measure or Quantity | Sodium (mgs.) |
|---|---|---|
| **MACARONI:** | | |
| Cooked: | | |
| 8–10 minutes, firm | 1 cup | 1 |
| 14–20 minutes, tender | 1 cup | 1 |
| Canned (Franco-American): | | |
| *Beefy Os* | 7 ½-oz. can | 1250 |
| *PizzOs* | 7 ½-oz. can | 1060 |
| Frozen: | | |
| (Banquet) & beef: | | |
| Regular | 12-oz. dinner | 2254 |
| *Buffet Supper* | 2-lb. pkg. | 5345 |
| (Morton) | 10-oz. dinner | 875 |
| (Swanson) | 12-oz. dinner | 925 |
| **MACARONI & CHEESE:** | | |
| Canned: | | |
| (Franco-American) regular or elbow | 7⅜-oz. serving | 960 |
| (Hormel) *Short Orders* | 7½-oz. can | 917 |
| Frozen: | | |
| (Banquet): | | |
| *Buffet Supper* | 2-lb. pkg. | 3484 |
| Casserole | 8-oz. pkg. | 930 |
| (Green Giant) *Boil 'N Bag* | 9-oz. entree | 1115 |
| (Morton) dinner | 11-oz. dinner | 905 |
| (Stouffer's) | 6-oz. serving | 780 |
| (Swanson) | 12-oz. entree | 1824 |
| (Van de Kamp's) | 5-oz. serving | 590 |
| Mix (Golden Grain) | ¼ pkg. | 430 |
| **MACARONI & CHEESE PIE,** | | |
| frozen (Swanson) | 7-oz. pie | 880 |
| ***MACARONI SHELLS & SAUCE** | | |
| (Lipton) creamy garlic | ½ cup | 535 |
| **MALTED MILK MIX** (Carnation): | | |
| Chocolate | 3 heaping tsps. | 47 |
| Natural | 3 heaping tsps. | 98 |

| Food and Description | Measure or Quantity | Sodium (mgs.) |
|---|---|---|
| MALT LIQUOR, *Champale*, regular | 12 fl. oz. | 64 |
| *MALT-O-MEAL*, cereal | 1 T. | Tr. |
| MANDARIN ORANGE (See TANGERINE) | | |
| MANGO, fresh | 1 med. mango | 9 |
| MANGO NECTAR (Libby's) | 6 fl. oz. | 5 |
| MANHATTAN COCKTAIL | | |
| (Mr. Boston) 20% alcohol | 3 fl. oz. | 4 |
| MAPLE SYRUP (See SYRUP, Maple) | | |
| MARGARINE: | | |
| Regular, salted | 1 pat (1″ × 1.3″ × 1″, 5 grams) | 49 |
| Regular, unsalted | 1 T. | 1 |
| (Mazola) salted | 1 T. | 104 |
| (Promise) soft or stick, salted | 1 T. | 96 |
| MARGARINE, IMITATION OR DIETETIC: | | |
| (Imperial) diet | 1 T. | 136 |
| (Mazola) | 1 T. | 130 |
| MARGARINE, WHIPPED | | |
| (Blue Bonnet; Imperial) | 1 T. | 70 |
| MARGARITA COCKTAIL (Mr. Boston): | | |
| Regular | 3 fl. oz. | 37 |
| Strawberry | 3 fl. oz. | 25 |
| MARINADE MIX: | | |
| Chicken (Adolph's) | 1-oz. packet | 4105 |
| Meat: | | |
| (Adolph's) | .8-oz. pkg. | 4636 |
| (Durkee) | 1-oz. pkg. | 4104 |
| (French's) | 1-oz. pkg. | 4320 |
| (Kikkoman) | 1-oz. pkg. | 4000 |
| MARJORAM (French's) | 1 tsp. | 1 |
| MARMALADE: | | |
| Sweetened | 1 T. | 3 |
| Dietetic: | | |
| (Dia-Mel) | 1 T. | <3 |
| (Featherweight) | 1 T. | 40-50 |
| (Louis Sherry) | 1 T. | <3 |
| *MARSHMALLOW FLUFF* | 1 heaping tsp. | 5 |
| *MARSHMALLOW KRISPIES*, cereal (Kellogg's) | 1¼ cup | 285 |
| MARTINI COCKTAIL (Mr. Boston) vodka, 20% alcohol | 3 fl. oz. | Tr. |
| *MASA HARINA* (Quaker) | ⅓ cup | 2 |
| *MASA TRIGO* (Quaker) | ⅓ cup | 294 |

| Food and Description | Measure or Quantity | Sodium (mgs.) |
|---|---|---|
| **MATZO** (Horowitz-Margareten) | | |
| regular | 1 matzo | Tr. |
| **MAYONNAISE:** | | |
| Real, *Hellman's* (Best Foods) | 1 T. (.5 oz.) | 80 |
| Imitation or dietetic: | | |
| (Dia-Mel) | 1 T. | 22 |
| (Diet Delight) *Mayo-Lite* | 1 T. | 75 |
| (Featherweight) *Soyamaise* | 1 T. | 3 |
| *MAYPO,* cereal: | | |
| 30-second | ¼ cup | 4 |
| Vermont style | ¼ cup | 7 |
| *McDONALD'S:* | | |
| *Big Mac* | 1 hamburger | 979 |
| Biscuit: | | |
| Plain | 1 piece | 786 |
| With bacon, egg & cheese | 1 sandwich | 1269 |
| With sausage & egg | 1 sandwich | 1301 |
| Cheeseburger | 1 cheeseburger | 743 |
| *Chicken McNuggets* | 1 serving | 512 |
| *Chicken McNugget Sauce:* | | |
| Barbecue | 1.1-oz. | 309 |
| Hot mustard | 1.1-oz. | 259 |
| Sweet & sour | 1.1-oz. | 186 |
| Cookies: | | |
| Chocolate chip | 1 package | 313 |
| *McDonaldland* | 1 package | 358 |
| *Egg McMuffin* | 1 serving | 885 |
| Egg, scrambled | 1 serving | 205 |
| English muffin, with butter | 1 muffin | 310 |
| *Filet-O-Fish* | 1 sandwich | 799 |
| Grapefruit juice | 6 fl. oz. | 2 |
| Hamburger | 1 hamburger | 505 |
| Hot cakes with butter & syrup | 1 serving | 1070 |
| Orange juice | 6 fl. oz. | 2 |
| Pie: | | |
| Apple | 1 pie | 398 |
| Cherry | 1 pie | 427 |
| Potato: | | |
| Fried | 1 regular order | 109 |
| Hash browns | 1 order | 325 |
| *Quarter Pounder:* | | |
| Regular | 1 hamburger | 718 |
| With cheese | 1 hamburger | 1220 |
| Sausage, pork | 1 serving | 423 |
| *Sausage McMuffin:* | | |
| Plain | 1 sandwich | 942 |
| With egg | 1 sandwich | 1044 |

| Food and Description | Measure or Quantity | Sodium (mgs.) |
|---|---|---|
| Shake: | | |
|    Chocolate | 1 serving | 300 |
|    Strawberry | 1 serving | 207 |
|    Vanilla | 1 serving | 201 |
| Sundae: | | |
|    Caramel | 1 serving | 145 |
|    Hot fudge | 1 serving | 170 |
|    Strawberry | 1 serving | 90 |
| **MEATBALL DINNER or ENTREE,** frozen: | | |
|    (Green Giant) twin pouch | 9-oz. entree | 820 |
|    (Swanson) | 8¼-oz. entree | 893 |
| **MEATBALL SEASONING MIX:** | | |
|    *(Durkee) Italian style | 1 cup | 1019 |
|    (French's) | 1.5-oz. pkg. | 3300 |
| **MEATBALL STEW,** frozen (Stouffer's) | | |
|    *Lean Cuisine* | 10-oz. pkg. | 1260 |
| **MEATBALLS, SWEDISH,** frozen | | |
|    (Stouffer's) with noodles | 11-oz. pkg. | 1620 |
| **MEAT LOAF DINNER,** frozen: | | |
|    (Banquet): | | |
|      American Favorites | 11-oz. dinner | 1525 |
|      Extra Helping | 19-oz. dinner | 2396 |
|    (Morton) Family Meal | 2-lb. pkg. | 4400 |
|    (Swanson): | | |
|      Regular | 11-oz. dinner | 1010 |
|      With tomato sauce & whipped potatoes | 9-oz. entree | 1020 |
| **MEAT LOAF SEASONING MIX** | | |
|    (French's) | 1.5-oz. pkg. | 4920 |
| **MEAT, POTTED** (Libby's) | ⅓ of 5-oz. can | 297 |
| **MEAT TENDERIZER** (Adolph's) | 1 tsp. | 1849 |
| **MELBA TOAST,** salted | | |
|    (Old London): | | |
|    Garlic, onion or white rounds | 1 piece | 22 |
|    Pumpernickel, rye, wheat or white, salted | 1 piece | 39 |
|    Sesame, flat | 1 piece | 49 |
| **MELON BALL,** in syrup, frozen | ½ cup | 10 |
| **MENUDO**(Hormel) *Casa Grande* | 7½-oz. can | 1097 |
| **MEXICAN DINNER,** frozen: | | |
|    (Banquet) International Favorites combination | 20-oz. dinner | 2510 |
|    (Morton) | 11-oz. dinner | 1242 |
|    (Swanson) 4-compartment | 16-oz. dinner | 1865 |
|    (Van de Kamp's) | 11½-oz. dinner | 1040 |

| Food and Description | Measure or Quantity | Sodium (mgs.) |
|---|---|---|
| **MILK BREAK BARS** (Pillsbury): | | |
| Chocolate or natural | 1 bar | 75 |
| Peanut butter | 1 bar | 115 |
| **MILK, CONDENSED** (Carnation) | 1 fl. oz. | 49 |
| **\*MILK, DRY,** non-fat, instant (Alba; | | |
| Carnation; *Sanalac*) | 1 cup | 120 |
| **MILK, EVAPORATED:** | | |
| Regular: | | |
| (Carnation) | 1 fl. oz. | 33 |
| (Pet) | ½ cup | 140 |
| Filled (Pet) | ½ cup | 150 |
| Low fat (Carnation) | 1 fl. oz. | 34 |
| Skimmed (Carnation) | 1 fl. oz. | 35 |
| **MILK, FRESH:** | | |
| Buttermilk (Friendship) | 8 fl. oz. | 125 |
| Chocolate | 8 fl. oz. | 118 |
| Skim | 1 cup | 127 |
| Whole | 1 cup | 122 |
| **MILK, GOAT,** whole | 1 cup | 83 |
| **MILK, HUMAN** | 1 oz. | 5 |
| *MILNOT*, dairy vegetable blend | 1 fl. oz. | 35 |
| **MINERAL WATER** (Schweppes) | 6 fl. oz. | 3 |
| *MINI-WHEATS*, cereal (Kellogg's) | 1 biscuit | <10 |
| **MINT LEAVES** | ½ oz. | Tr. |
| **MOLASSES:** | | |
| Blackstrap | 1 T. | 18 |
| Light | 1 T. | 3 |
| Medium | 1 T. | 7 |
| Unsulphured (Grandma's) | 1 T. | 8 |
| *MOST*, cereal (Kellogg's) | ½ cup | 30 |
| MSG (Durkee) | 1 tsp. | 30 |
| **MUFFIN:** | | |
| Blueberry: | | |
| (Morton) rounds | 1 ½-oz. muffin | 180 |
| (Pepperidge Farm) regular | | |
| or frozen | 1.9-oz. muffin | 259 |
| Bran (Arnold) *Bran'nola* | 2.3-oz. muffin | 260 |
| Corn: | | |
| (Morton) | 1.7-oz. muffin | 280 |
| (Pepperidge Farm) | 1.9-oz. muffin | 260 |
| (Thomas') | 2-oz. muffin | 330 |
| English: | | |
| (Arnold) extra crisp | 2.3-oz. muffin | 310 |
| (Pepperidge Farm): | | |
| Plain | 2-oz. muffin | 365 |
| Cinnamon apple | 2-oz. muffin | 350 |
| Sourdough | 2-oz. muffin | 345 |

| Food and Description | Measure or Quantity | Sodium (mgs.) |
|---|---|---|
| Wheat | 2-oz. muffin | 340 |
| (Thomas') regular | 2-oz. muffin | 207 |
| (Wonder) | 2-oz. muffin | 284 |
| Orange-cranberry (Pepperidge Farm) | 2.1-oz. muffin | 200 |
| Plain | 1.4-oz. muffin | 176 |
| Raisin (Arnold) | 2.5-oz. muffin | 350 |
| Sourdough (Wonder) | 2-oz. muffin | 128 |
| **MUFFIN MIX:** | | |
| *Blueberry (Betty Crocker) wild | 1 muffin | 150 |
| Bran: | | |
| (Duncan Hines) | ½12 of pkg. | 97 |
| (Elam's) | 1 T. | 43 |
| *Cherry (Betty Crocker) | ½12 of pkg. | 120 |
| Corn: | | |
| *(Betty Crocker) | 1 muffin | 315 |
| *(Flako) | 1 muffin | 370 |
| **MUSCATEL WINE** (Gold Seal) | 3 fl. oz. | 3 |
| **MUSHROOM:** | | |
| Raw, whole | ½ lb. | 33 |
| Raw, trimmed, sliced | ½ cup | 5 |
| Canned, solids & liq.: | | |
| (Green Giant): | | |
| Regular | 2-oz. serving | 260 |
| In butter sauce | ½ of 3½-oz. can | 293 |
| (Shady Oaks) | 4-oz. can | 452 |
| Frozen (Green Giant) whole, in butter sauce | ½ cup | 240 |
| **MUSHROOM, CHINESE,** dried | 1 oz. | 11 |
| **MUSSEL,** meat only | 1 lb. (weighed in shell) | 380 |
| **MUSTARD:** | | |
| Powder (French's) | 1 tsp. | Tr. |
| Prepared: | | |
| Brown (French's) | 1 tsp. | 48 |
| Dijon, *Grey Poupon* | 1 tsp. | 149 |
| Horseradish (Nalley's) | 1 tsp. | 88 |
| Yellow | 1 tsp. | 113 |
| **MUSTARD GREENS:** | | |
| Canned (Sunshine) solids & liq. | ½ cup | 371 |
| Frozen: | | |
| (Birds Eye) | ⅓ pkg. | 27 |
| (Southland) | ⅓ 16-oz. pkg. | 20 |

# N

| Food and Description | Measure or Quantity | Sodium (mgs.) |
|---|---|---|
| **NATURAL CEREAL:** | | |
| (Familia): | | |
| Regular | ½ cup | 8 |
| Bran | ½ cup | 90 |
| No added salt | ½ cup | 2 |
| *Heartland* (Pet) | ¼ cup | 80 |
| (Quaker): | | |
| Hot, whole wheat | ⅓ | 1 |
| 100% natural, with apple & cinamon | ¼ cup | 15 |
| **NATURE SNACKS** (Sun-Maid): | | |
| Carob Crunch | 1 oz. | 13 |
| Carob Peanut | 1¼ oz. | 16 |
| Raisin Crunch | 1 oz. | 41 |
| Rocky Road | 1 oz. | 4 |
| Yogurt Crunch | 1 oz. | 28 |
| Yogurt Peanuts | 1¼ oz. | 25 |
| **NECTARINE**, flesh only | 4 oz. | 7 |
| **NOODLE:** | | |
| Dry, 1½" strips | 1 oz. | 1 |
| Cooked, 1½" strips | 1 cup | 3 |
| **NOODLES & BEEF:** | | |
| Canned (Hormel) *Short Orders* | 7½-oz. can | 974 |
| Frozen (Banquet) *Buffet Supper* | 2-lb. pkg. | 5581 |
| **NOODLES & CHICKEN:** | | |
| Canned (Hormel) *Dinty Moore, Short Orders* | 7½-oz. can | 1144 |
| Frozen (Swanson) | 10½-oz. dinner | 805 |
| **NOODLE, CHOW MEIN** (La Choy) | ½ cup (1 oz.) | 205 |
| ***NOODLE MIX:** | | |
| (Betty Crocker): | | |
| Fettucini Alfredo | ¼ pkg. | 490 |
| Stroganoff | ¼ pkg. | 605 |
| (Lipton): | | |
| Regular: | | |
| Beef | ½ cup | 595 |

| Food and Description | Measure or Quantity | Sodium (mgs.) |
|---|---|---|
| Butter | ½ cup | 565 |
| Cheese | ½ cup | 540 |
| Sour cream & chive | ½ cup | 455 |
| Deluxe: | | |
| Alfredo | ½ cup | 560 |
| Parmesano | ½ cup | 445 |
| Stroganoff | ½ cup | 510 |
| *NOODLE, RAMEN (La Choy) | | |
| canned: | | |
| Beef | ½ of 3-oz. can | 1040 |
| Chicken | ½ of 3-oz. can | 1159 |
| Oriental | ½ of 3-oz. can | 742 |
| NOODLE, RICE (La Choy) | 1 oz. | 360 |
| NOODLE ROMANOFF, frozen (Stouffer's) | ⅓ pkg. | 675 |
| NUT, MIXED: | | |
| Dry roasted: | | |
| (Flavor House) salted | 1 oz. | 81 |
| (Planters) salted | 1 oz. | 222 |
| Oil roasted (Planters) with or without peanuts, salted | 1 oz. | 219 |
| NUTMEG (French's) | 1 tsp. | Tr. |
| NUTRI-GRAIN, cereal (Kellogg's): | | |
| Corn | ½ cup | 185 |
| Wheat | ⅔ cup | 195 |
| Wheat & raisins | ⅔ cup | 165 |

# O

| Food and Description | Measure or Quantity | Sodium (mgs.) |
|---|---|---|
| **OAT FLAKES,** cereal (Post) | ⅔ cup | 254 |
| **OATMEAL:** | | |
| Dry: | | |
| Regular: | | |
| (Elam's) Scotch style | 1 oz. | 3 |
| (H-O) old fashioned | 1 T. | Tr. |
| (Quaker),old fashioned | ⅓ cup | 1 |
| Instant: | | |
| (Harvest Brand) apple | | |
| & cinnamon | 1¼-oz. pkg. | 242 |
| (H-O): | | |
| Regular, boxed | 1 T. | Tr. |
| With bran & spice | 1½-oz. packet | 297 |
| With cinnamon & spice | 1.6-oz. packet | 306 |
| With maple & brown sugar | | |
| flavor | 1½-oz. packet | 286 |
| (Quaker): | | |
| Regular | 1-oz. packet | 281 |
| Apple & cinnamon | 1¼-oz. packet | 181 |
| Bran & raisin | 1⅝-oz. packet | 258 |
| Raisins & spice | 1½-oz. packet | 217 |
| (3-Minute Brand) | ½ cup | 341 |
| Quick: | | |
| (Harvest Brand) | ⅓ cup | <5 |
| (H-O) | ½ cup | Tr. |
| (Ralston Purina) | ⅓ cup | 3 |
| (3-Minute Brand) | ⅓ cup | <5 |
| Cooked, regular | 1 cup | 523 |
| **OIL, SALAD OR COOKING** | Any quantity | 0 |
| **OKRA:** | | |
| Raw, whole | 1 lb. | 12 |
| Frozen: | | |
| (Birds Eye) whole | ⅓ pkg. | 2 |
| (Southland) cut | ⅓ of 16-oz. pkg. | 2 |

| Food and Description | Measure or Quantity | Sodium (mgs.) |
|---|---|---|
| **OLIVE:** | | |
| Green | 4 med. or 3 extra large or 2 giant | 384 |
| Ripe, Mission | 3 small or 2 large | 75 |
| **OMELET,** frozen (Swanson) *TV Brand:* | | |
| With cheese sauce & ham | 7-oz. entree | 1305 |
| Spanish style | 7¾-oz. entree | 905 |
| **ONION:** | | |
| Raw | 2½" onion | 10 |
| Boiled, pearl onion | ½ cup (3.2 oz.) | 6 |
| Canned (Durkee) *O & C:* | | |
| Boiled | ¼ of 16-oz. jar. | 8 |
| Creamed | 1-oz. serving | 2854 |
| Dehydrated (Gilroy) flakes | 1 tsp. | Tr. |
| Frozen: | | |
| (Birds Eye): | | |
| Chopped | 1 oz. | 2 |
| Creamed | ⅓ pkg. | 333 |
| Whole | 4 oz. | 10 |
| (Green Giant) in cheese sauce | ½ cup | 400 |
| (Mrs. Paul's) french-fried rings | ½ of 5-oz. pkg. | 305 |
| (Southland) chopped | ⅕ of 10-oz. pkg. | 2 |
| **ONION BOUILLON:** | | |
| (Herb-Ox) | 1 cube | 560 |
| *MBT* | 1 packet | 795 |
| **ONION, COCKTAIL** (Vlasic) | 1 oz. | 371 |
| **ONION, GREEN** | 1 small onion | Tr. |
| **ONION SALAD SEASONING** | | |
| (French's) instant | 1 T. | 2 |
| **ONION SALT** (French's) | 1 tsp. | 1620 |
| **ONION SOUP** (See SOUP, Onion) | | |
| **ORANGE:** | | |
| Peeled | ½ cup | 1 |
| Sections | 4 oz. | 1 |
| **ORANGE DRINK:** | | |
| Canned: | | |
| *Capri Sun* | 6¾-fl.-oz. can | 2 |
| (Hi-C) | 6 fl. oz. | 58 |
| *Mix: | | |
| Regular (Hi-C) | 6 fl. oz. | 1 |
| Dietetic, *Crystal Light* | 6 fl. oz. | Tr. |
| **ORANGE-GRAPEFRUIT JUICE:** | | |
| Canned (Del Monte) unsweetened | 6 fl. oz. | 2 |
| *Frozen (Minute Maid) unsweetened | 6 fl. oz. | Tr. |
| **ORANGE JUICE:** | | |
| Canned: | | |
| (Del Monte) unsweetened | 6 fl. oz. | <10 |

| Food and Description | Measure or Quantity | Sodium (mgs.) |
|---|---|---|
| (Libby's) unsweetened | 6 fl. oz. | 5 |
| (Texsun) sweetened | 6 fl. oz. | 2 |
| Chilled (Minute Maid) | 6 fl. oz. | 1 |
| *Frozen: | | |
| (Birds Eye) *Orange Plus* | 6 fl. oz. | 9 |
| (Snow Crop) | 6 fl. oz. | 1 |
| (Sunkist) | 6 fl. oz. | Tr. |
| **ORANGE JUICE BAR** | | |
| (Sunkist) | 3-fl.-oz. bar | 5 |
| **ORANGE-PINEAPPLE JUICE,** | | |
| canned (Texsun) | 8 fl. oz. | 2 |
| *OVALTINE*, chocolate | ¾ oz. | 146 |
| *OVEN FRY* (General Foods): | | |
| Crispy crumb for pork | 4.2-oz. envelope | 2780 |
| Crispy crumb for chicken | 4.2-oz. envelope | 827 |
| Home style flour recipe | 3.2-oz. envelope | 3955 |
| **OYSTER:** | | |
| Raw, Eastern | 19-31 small or 13-19 med. | 175 |
| Fried | 4 oz. | 234 |
| **OYSTER STEW,** home recipe | ½ cup | 407 |

# P

| Food and<br>Description | Measure or<br>Quantity | Sodium<br>(mgs.) |
|---|---|---|
| **PAC-MAN CEREAL** (General Mills) | 1 cup | 195 |
| ***PANCAKE BATTER,** frozen | | |
| (Aunt Jemima): | | |
| Plain | 4″ pancake | 286 |
| Blueberry | 4″ pancake | 233 |
| Buttermilk | 4″ pancake | 244 |
| **PANCAKE & SAUSAGE,** frozen | | |
| (Swanson) | 6 oz. entree | 950 |
| ***PANCAKE & WAFFLE MIX:** | | |
| Plain: | | |
| (Aunt Jemima): | | |
| Complete | 4″ pancake | 290 |
| Original | 4″ pancake | 183 |
| (Log Cabin): | | |
| Complete | 4″ pancake | 203 |
| Original | 4″ pancake | 180 |
| (Pillsbury) *Hungry Jack:* | | |
| Complete, bulk | 4″ pancake | 243 |
| *Extra Lights* | 4″ pancake | 162 |
| *Golden Blend,* complete | 4″ pancake | 305 |
| *Panshakes* | 4″ pancake | 293 |
| Blueberry (Pillsbury) *Hungry Jack* | 4″ pancake | 272 |
| Buckwheat (Aunt Jemima) | 4″ pancake | 173 |
| Buttermilk: | | |
| (Aunt Jemima): | | |
| Regular | 4″ pancake | 330 |
| Complete | 4″ pancake | 290 |
| (Pillsbury) *Hungry Jack,* complete | 4″ pancake | 243 |
| Whole wheat (Aunt Jemima) | 4″ pancake | 242 |
| Dietetic: | | |
| (Dia-Mel) | 3″ pancake | 58 |
| (Featherweight) | 4″ pancake | 23 |
| **PANCAKE & WAFFLE SYRUP** | | |
| (see SYRUP, Pancake & Waffle) | | |

| Food and Description | Measure or Quantity | Sodium (mgs.) |
|---|---|---|
| **PAPAYA,** fresh: | | |
| Cubed | ½ cup | 3 |
| Juice | 4 oz. | 35 |
| **PAPRIKA** (French's) | 1 tsp. | Tr. |
| **PARSLEY:** | | |
| Fresh, chopped | 1 T. | 2 |
| Dried (French's) | 1 tsp. | 6 |
| **PASTINAS,** egg | 1 oz. | 1 |
| **PASTRAMI** (Eckrich) sliced | 1-oz. serving | 360 |
| **PASTRY SHEET, PUFF,** frozen (Pepperidge Farm) | 1 sheet | 580 |
| **PASTRY SHELL,** frozen (Pepperidge Farm) | 1 shell | 180 |
| **PATÉ,** liver (Sell's) | ½ of 4.8-oz. can | 571 |
| **PEA,** green: | | |
| Boiled, without salt | ½ cup | Tr. |
| Canned, regular pack, solids & liq.: | | |
| (Comstock) | ½ cup | 400 |
| (Del Monte) early | ½ cup | 355 |
| (Green Giant): | | |
| Early, with onions | ½ cup | 535 |
| Sweet | ½ cup | 375 |
| Sweet, with onions | ½ cup | 665 |
| (Larsen) *Freshlike* | ½ cup | 320 |
| (Le Sueur) early June | ½ cup | 375 |
| (Libby's) sweet | ½ cup | 337 |
| Canned, dietetic pack, solids & liq.: | | |
| (Del Monte) No Salt Added | ½ cup | <10 |
| (Diet Delight) | ½ cup | 5 |
| (Featherweight) sweet | ½ cup | <10 |
| (Larsen) *Fresh-Lite* | ½ cup | 13 |
| Frozen: | | |
| (Birds Eye): | | |
| Regular | ⅓ pkg. | 131 |
| In butter sauce | ⅓ pkg. | 641 |
| In cream sauce | ⅓ pkg. | 446 |
| Tiny | ⅓ pkg. | 121 |
| With sliced mushrooms | ⅓ pkg. | 75 |
| (Green Giant): | | |
| Creamed | ½ cup | 320 |
| Early & sweet in butter sauce | ½ cup | 490 |
| Sweet, *Harvest Fresh* | 4 oz. | 280 |
| (Mc Kenzie) tiny | 3.3-oz. serving | 127 |
| **PEA & CARROT:** | | |
| Canned, regular pack, solids & liq.: | | |
| (Comstock) | ½ cup | 430 |
| (Del Monte) | ½ cup | 355 |

| Food and Description | Measure or Quantity | Sodium (mgs.) |
|---|---|---|
| (Larsen) *Freshlike* | ½ cup | 340 |
| (Libby's) | ½ cup | 315 |
| Canned, dietetic pack, solids & liq.: | | |
| (Diet Delight) | ½ cup | 5 |
| (Larsen) *Fresh-Lite* | ½ cup | 33 |
| (S&W) *Nutradiet* | ½ cup | <10 |
| Frozen: | | |
| (Birds Eye) | ⅓ pkg. | 92 |
| (McKenzie) | 3.3-oz. serving | 75 |
| **PEA, CROWDER,** frozen | | |
| (Birds Eye) | ⅕ of 16-oz. pkg. | 6 |
| **PEA POD,** frozen (La Choy) | 6-oz. pkg. | <20 |
| **PEA PUREE** (Larsen) | ½ cup | 7 |
| **PEACH:** | | |
| Fresh, with thin skin | 2″ peach | 1 |
| Fresh, slices | ½ cup | 1 |
| Canned, regular pack, solids & liq.: | | |
| (Del Monte) cling | ½ cup | <10 |
| (Libby's) heavy syrup: | | |
| Halves | ½ cup | 9 |
| Sliced | ½ cup | 10 |
| Canned, dietetic pack, solids & liq.: | | |
| (Del Monte) Lite, Cling | ½ cup | <10 |
| (Diet Delight) Cling, juice pack | ½ cup | 10 |
| (Featherweight) | ½ cup | 10 |
| (Libby's) Lite, water pack | ½ cup | 10 |
| Dried (Sun-Maid/Sunsweet) | 3 oz. | 3 |
| Frozen (Birds Eye) | 5-oz. serving | 9 |
| **PEACH BUTTER** (Smucker's) | 1 T. | 2 |
| **PEACH DRINK** (Hi-C): | | |
| Canned | 6 fl. oz. | Tr. |
| *Mix | 6 fl. oz. | 17 |
| **PEACH NECTAR,** canned (Libby's) | 6 fl. oz. | 5 |
| **PEACH PRESERVE OR JAM:** | | |
| Sweetened (Smucker's) | 1 T. | 4 |
| Dietetic (Featherweight) artificially sweetened | 1 T. | 40-50 |
| **PEANUT:** | | |
| Raw, in shell | 1 lb. | 17 |
| Dry roasted: | | |
| (Fisher) unsalted | 1 oz. | 1 |
| (Planters) salted | 1 oz. | 222 |
| (Tom's) salted | 1 oz. | 170 |
| Oil roasted (Planters) salted | 1 oz. | 219 |
| **PEANUT BUTTER:** | | |
| Regular: | | |
| (Adam's) | 1 T. | 65 |

| Food and Description | Measure or Quantity | Sodium (mgs.) |
|---|---|---|
| (Elam's) natural | 1 T. | 4 |
| (Jif) creamy | 1 T. | 89 |
| (Laura Scrudder's) | 1 T. | 62 |
| (Peter Pan): | | |
| Crunchy | 1 T. | 59 |
| Smooth | 1 T. | 92 |
| (Skippy): | | |
| Creamy | 1 T. | 80 |
| Creamy, old fashioned | 1 T. | 75 |
| Dietetic: | | |
| (Adam's) | 1 T. | <3 |
| (Featherweight) low sodium | 1 T. | <5 |
| (Peter Pan) low sodium | 1 T. | Tr. |
| (S&W) *Nutradiet,* low sodium | 1 T. | <10 |
| **PEANUT BUTTER BAKING CHIPS** (Reese's) | 3 T. (1 oz.) | 55 |
| **PEAR:** | | |
| Whole | 3" × 2½" pear | 3 |
| Canned, regular pack, solids & liq.: | | |
| (Del Monte) Bartlett | ½ cup | <10 |
| (Libby's) | ½ cup | 6 |
| Canned, dietetic pack, solids & liq.: | | |
| (Del Monte) Lite | ½ cup | <10 |
| (Diet Delight) | ½ cup | 5 |
| (Featherweight) Bartlett | ½ cup | <10 |
| (Libby's) water pack | ½ cup | 10 |
| Dried (Sun-Maid) | ½ cup | 7 |
| **PEAR NECTAR,** canned (Libby's) | 6 fl. oz. | 5 |
| **PEAR-PASSION FRUIT NECTAR,** canned (Libby's) | 6 fl. oz. | 5 |
| *PEBBLES,* cereal: | | |
| Cocoa | ⅞ cup | 136 |
| Fruity | ⅞ cup | 158 |
| **PECAN:** | | |
| Halves | 6-7 pieces | 48 |
| Roasted, dry, salted: | | |
| (Fisher) | 1 oz. | 110 |
| (Planters) | 1 oz. | 222 |
| **PECTIN, FRUIT:** | | |
| *Certo* | 6-oz. pkg. | 5 |
| *Sure-Jell,* regular | 1¾-oz. pkg. | 12 |
| **PEPPER:** | | |
| Black (French's) | 1 tsp. | Tr. |
| Seasoned (French's) | 1 tsp. | 5 |
| **PEPPER, CHERRY** (Vlasic) mild | 1 oz. | 416 |
| **PEPPER, CHILI,** canned: | | |
| (Del Monte): | | |
| Green, whole | ½ cup | 819 |

| Food and Description | Measure or Quantity | Sodium (mgs.) |
|---|---|---|
| Jalapeno or chili, whole (Ortega): | ½ cup | 1653 |
| Diced, strips or whole | 1 oz. | 20 |
| Jalapeno, diced or whole | 1 oz. | 6 |
| (Vlasic) | 1 oz. | 386 |
| **PEPPERONCINI** (Vlasic) | | |
| Greek, mild | 1 oz. | 457 |
| **PEPPERONI:** | | |
| (Hormel): | | |
| Regular | 1 oz. | 462 |
| Leoni Brand | 1 oz. | 508 |
| Packaged, sliced | 1 slice | 140 |
| (Swift) | 1-oz. serving | 579 |
| **PEPPER STEAK,** frozen: | | |
| (Le Menu) | 11½-oz. dinner | 1062 |
| (Stouffer's) | 5½-oz. serving | 750 |
| **PEPPER, STUFFED:** | | |
| Home recipe | 2¾" × 2½" pepper with 1⅛ cups stuffing | 581 |
| Frozen: | | |
| (Green Giant) green, baked | ½ pkg. | 785 |
| (Stouffer's) | ½ of 15½-oz. pkg. | 960 |
| (Weight Watchers) with veal stuffing | 11¾-oz. meal | 1125 |
| **PEPPER, SWEET:** | | |
| Raw, green: | | |
| Whole | 1 lb. | 48 |
| Without stem & seeds | 1 med. pepper (2.6 oz.) | 8 |
| Boiled, green, without salt, drained | 1 med. pepper (2.6 oz.) | 7 |
| Frozen: | | |
| (McKenzie) | 1-oz. serving | 6 |
| (Southland), green | 2-oz. serving | 1 |
| **PERCH, OCEAN:** | | |
| Atlantic, raw: | | |
| Whole | 1 lb. | 111 |
| Meat only | 4 oz. | 71 |
| Pacific, raw, whole | 1 lb. | 77 |
| Frozen: | | |
| (Banquet) | 8¾-oz. dinner | 1416 |
| (Mrs. Paul's) fillet, breaded & fried | 2-oz. piece | 240 |
| (Van de Kamp's) *Today's Catch* | 4-oz. serving | 180 |
| **PERSIMMON:** | | |
| Japanese or Kaki, fresh: | | |
| With seeds | 4.4-oz. piece | 6 |

| Food and Description | Measure or Quantity | Sodium (mgs.) |
|---|---|---|
| Seedless | 4.4-oz. piece | 6 |
| Native, fresh, flesh only | 4-oz. serving | 1 |
| **PICKLE:** | | |
| Cucumber, fresh or bread & butter: | | |
| (Fannings) | 1.2-oz. serving | 189 |
| (Featherweight) low sodium | 1-oz. pickle | 3 |
| (Vlasic): | | |
| Chips, sweet butter | 1 oz. | 163 |
| Stix, sweet butter | 1 oz. | 112 |
| Dill: | | |
| (Featherweight) low sodium, whole | 1-oz. serving | <5 |
| (Smucker's) hamburger, sliced | 1 slice | 47 |
| (Vlasic): | | |
| Regular | 1 oz. | 381 |
| No garlic | 1 oz. | 213 |
| Hot & spicy (Vlasic) | 1 oz. | 386 |
| Kosher dill: | | |
| (Claussen) halves or whole | 2-oz. serving | 599 |
| (Featherweight) low sodium | 1-oz. serving | <5 |
| (Smucker's) whole | 2½" long pickle | 642 |
| (Vlasic): | | |
| Baby or gherkins | 1 oz. | 213 |
| Crunchy, half the salt | 1 oz. | 128 |
| Deli | 1 oz. | 178 |
| Spear, half the salt | 1 oz. | 122 |
| Sweet: | | |
| (Nalley's) *Nubbins* | 1-oz. serving | 28 |
| (Smucker's) whole | 2½" long pickle | 119 |
| (Vlasic) butter chips, half the salt | 1 oz. | 82 |
| Sweet & sour (Claussen) slices | 1 slice | 25 |
| **PIE:** | | |
| Regular, non-frozen: | | |
| Apple: | | |
| Home recipe, two crust | ⅙ of 9" pie | 476 |
| (Hostess) | 4½-oz. pie | 540 |
| Banana, home recipe, cream or custard | ⅙ of 9" pie | 295 |
| Berry, (Hostess) | 4½-oz. pie | 490 |
| Blackberry, home recipe, two crust | ⅙ of 9" pie | 423 |
| Blueberry: | | |
| Home recipe, two-crust | ⅙ of 9" pie | 423 |
| (Hostess) | 4½-oz. pie | 450 |
| Boston cream, home recipe | 1/12 of 8" pie | 128 |
| Butterscotch, home recipe, one-crust | ⅙ of 9" pie | 325 |

| Food and Description | Measure or Quantity | Sodium (mgs.) |
|---|---|---|
| Cherry: | | |
| Home recipe, two-crust | ⅙ of 9″ pie | 480 |
| (Hostess) | 4½-oz. pie | 530 |
| Chocolate chiffon, home recipe | ⅙ of 9″ pie | 353 |
| Chocolate meringue, home recipe | ⅙ of 9″ pie | 358 |
| Coconut custard, home recipe | ⅙ of 9″ pie | 375 |
| Lemon (Hostess) | 4½-oz. pie | 470 |
| Mince, home recipe, two-crust | ⅙ of 9″ pie | 708 |
| Peach (Hostess) | 4½-oz. pie | 445 |
| Pumpkin, home recipe, one-crust | ⅙ of 9″ pie | 325 |
| Raisin, home recipe, two-crust | ⅙ of 9″ pie | 450 |
| Strawberry (Hostess) | 4½-oz. pie | 400 |
| Frozen: | | |
| Apple: | | |
| (Banquet): | | |
| Regular | 8-oz. pie | 598 |
| Family size | ⅙ of 20-oz. pie | 282 |
| (Morton): | | |
| Regular | ⅙ of 24-oz. pie | 240 |
| *Great Little Desserts*, regular | 8-oz. pie | 510 |
| (Sara Lee) regular | ⅙ of 31-oz. pie | 280 |
| Banana (Morton) | ⅙ of 14-oz. pie | 130 |
| Banana cream: | | |
| (Banquet) | ⅙ of 14-oz. pie | 146 |
| (Morton) *Great Little Desserts* | 3½-oz. pie | 200 |
| Blackberry (Banquet) | ⅙ of 20-oz. pie | 342 |
| Blueberry: | | |
| (Banquet) | ⅙ of 20-oz. pie | 342 |
| (Morton) *Great Little Desserts* | 8-oz. pie | 525 |
| (Sara Lee) | ⅕ of 31-oz. pie | 220 |
| Cherry: | | |
| (Banquet) family size | ⅙ of 20-oz. pie | 258 |
| (Morton) regular | ⅙ of 24-oz. pie | 240 |
| (Sara Lee) | ⅙ of 31-oz. pie | 233 |
| Chocolate (Morton) | ⅙ of 14-oz. pie | 140 |
| Chocolate cream: | | |
| (Banquet) | ⅙ of 14-oz. pie | 106 |
| (Morton) *Great Little Desserts* | 3½-oz. pie | 200 |
| Coconut cream (Banquet) | ⅙ of 14-oz. pie | 113 |
| Coconut custard (Morton) | | |
| *Great Little Desserts* | 6½-oz. pie | 495 |
| Lemon cream: | | |
| (Banquet) | ⅙ of 14-oz. pie | 111 |
| (Morton) *Great Little Desserts* | 3½-oz. pie | 200 |
| Mince: | | |
| (Banquet) | ⅙ of 20-oz. pie | 364 |
| (Morton) | ⅙ of 24-oz. pie | 355 |

| Food and Description | Measure or Quantity | Sodium (mgs.) |
|---|---|---|
| Peach (Sara Lee) | ⅙ of 31-oz. pie | 253 |
| Pumpkin: | | |
| (Banquet) | ⅙ of 20-oz. pie | 341 |
| (Morton) | ⅙ of 24-oz. pie | 310 |
| (Sara Lee) | ⅛ of 45-oz. pie | 403 |
| Strawberry cream: | | |
| (Banquet) | ⅙ of 14-oz. pie | 112 |
| (Morton) | ⅙ of 16-oz. pie | 122 |
| **PIECRUST:** | | |
| Home recipe, 9″ pie | 1 crust | 1100 |
| Frozen (Banquet) 9″ shell: | | |
| Regular | 1 crust | 960 |
| Deep Dish | 1 crust | 936 |
| Refrigerated (Pillsbury) | 2-crust shell | 2200 |
| **\*PIECRUST MIX:** | | |
| (Betty Crocker): | | |
| Regular | 1/16 pkg. | 140 |
| Stick | ⅛ of stick | 140 |
| (Flako) | ⅙ of 9″ pie shell | 314 |
| (Pillsbury) mix or stick | ⅙ of 2-crust pie | 425 |
| **PIE FILLING** (See also | | |
| PUDDING OR PIE FILLING): | | |
| Apple (Comstock) | ⅙ of 21-oz. can | 150 |
| Apple rings or slices | | |
| (See APPLE, canned) | | |
| Apricot (Comstock) | ⅙ of 21-oz. can | 250 |
| Banana cream (Comstock) | ⅙ of 21-oz. can | 700 |
| Blueberry (Comstock) | ⅙ of 21-oz. can | 350 |
| Coconut cream (Comstock) | ⅙ of 21-oz. can | 400 |
| Coconut custard, home recipe, made with egg yolk & milk | 5 oz. (inc. crust) | 334 |
| Lemon (Comstock) | ⅙ of 21-oz. can | 300 |
| Pumpkin (Libby's) (See also PUMPKIN, canned) | 1 cup | 420 |
| Raisin (Comstock) | ⅙ of 21-oz. can | 200 |
| **\*PIE MIX** (Betty Crocker) | | |
| Boston cream | ⅛ of pie | 405 |
| **PIEROGIES,** frozen (Mrs. Paul's) potato & cheese | 1 pierogi | 240 |
| **PIMIENTO,** canned (Sunshine) diced or sliced | 1 T. | 3 |
| **PINA COLADA** (Mr. Boston) 12½% alcohol | 3 fl. oz. | 29 |
| **PINEAPPLE:** | | |
| Fresh, slices | 1 slice (¾″ × 3½″) | Tr. |
| Canned, regular pack, solids & liq.: | | |
| (Del Monte) slices, medium | ½ cup | <10 |

| Food and Description | Measure or Quantity | Sodium (mgs.) |
|---|---|---|
| (Dole): | | |
| Juice pack, chunk, crushed or sliced | ½ cup | 1 |
| Heavy syrup, chunk, crushed or sliced | ½ cup | 2 |
| Canned, unsweetened or dietetic, solids & liq.: | | |
| (Diet Delight) juice pack | ½ cup | 5 |
| (Libby's) Lite | ½ cup | 10 |
| **PINEAPPLE & GRAPEFRUIT JUICE DRINK,** canned: | | |
| (Del Monte) regular or pink | 6 fl. oz. | 50 |
| (Dole) pink | 6 fl. oz. | Tr. |
| (Texsun) | 6 fl. oz. | 2 |
| **PINEAPPLE JUICE:** | | |
| Canned: | | |
| (Del Monte) | 6 fl. oz. | <10 |
| (Dole) | 6 fl. oz. | 2 |
| (Texsun) | 6 fl. oz. | 2 |
| *Frozen (Minute Maid) | 6 fl. oz. | 2 |
| **PINEAPPLE-ORANGE JUICE:** | | |
| Canned (Del Monte) | 6 fl. oz. | 20 |
| *Frozen (Minute Maid) | 6 fl. oz. | 2 |
| **PINEAPPLE PRESERVE OR JAM,** sweetened (Smucker's) | 1 T. | 2 |
| **PISTACHIO NUT** (Fisher) shelled, roasted, salted | 1 oz. | 100 |
| **PIZZA PIE:** | | |
| Regular, non-frozen: | | |
| Home recipe, with cheese topping | ⅛ of 14" pie | 527 |
| (Pizza Hut): | | |
| Cheese | ½ of 10" pie | 1431 |
| Pepperoni | ½ of 10" pie | 1638 |
| Frozen: | | |
| Cheese: | | |
| (Celeste) | ¼ of 19-oz. pie | 803 |
| (Stouffer's) French Bread | ½ of 10⅜-oz. pkg. | 850 |
| (Weight Watchers) | 6-oz. pie | 740 |
| Combination: | | |
| (Celeste) Chicago style | ¼ of 24-oz. pie | 1156 |
| (La Pizzeria) | ½ of 13½-oz. pie | 959 |
| (Van de Kamp's) thick crust | ¼ of 23½-oz. pie | 614 |
| (Weight Watchers) deluxe | 7¼-oz. pie | 850 |
| Deluxe: | | |
| (Celeste) | 9-oz. pie | 1589 |
| (Stouffer's) French Bread | ½ of 12⅜-oz. pkg. | 1150 |

| Food and Description | Measure or Quantity | Sodium (mgs.) |
|---|---|---|
| Hamburger (Stouffer's) French Bread | ½ of 12¼-oz. pkg. | 1100 |
| Mexican style (Van de Kamp's) | ½ of 11-oz. pkg. | 569 |
| Mushroom (Stouffer's) French Bread | ½ of 12-oz. pkg. | 1755 |
| Pepperoni: | | |
| (Celeste regular) | ¼ of 20-oz. pie | 1082 |
| (Stouffer's) French Bread | ½ of 11½-oz. pkg. | 1190 |
| (Van de Kamp's) | ¼ of 22-oz. pie | 651 |
| Sausage: | | |
| (Celeste) | 8-oz. pie | 1528 |
| (Stouffer's) French Bread | ½ of 12-oz. pkg. | 1320 |
| (Weight Watchers) veal | 6¾-oz. pie | 934 |
| Sausage & mushroom: | | |
| (Celeste) | ¼ of 24-oz. pie | 1195 |
| (Stouffer's) French Bread | ½ of 12½-oz. pkg. | 1220 |
| Sicilian style (Celeste) deluxe | ¼ of 26-oz. pie | 1190 |
| Vegetable (Weight Watchers) | 7¼-oz. pie | 835 |
| **PIZZA SAUCE** (Contadina): | | |
| Regular | ½ cup | 790 |
| With cheese | ½ cup | 760 |
| With pepperoni | ½ cup | 720 |
| **PLUM:** | | |
| Fresh, Japanese & hybrid | 2″ plum | Tr. |
| Fresh, prune-type, halves | ½ cup | Tr. |
| Canned, regular pack (Stokely-Van Camp) | ½ cup | 28 |
| Canned, unsweetened, purple, solids & liq.: | | |
| (Diet Delight) juice pack | ½ cup | 5 |
| (Featherweight) | ½ cup | <10 |
| **PLUM PRESERVE OR JAM,** sweetened (Smucker's) | 1 T. | 3 |
| **PLUM PUDDING,** canned (Richardson & Robbins) | 2″ wedge | 150 |
| **POLYNESIAN-STYLE DINNER,** frozen (Swanson) | 12-oz. dinner | 1355 |
| **POMEGRANTE,** whole | 1 lb. | 8 |
| **PONDEROSA RESTAURANT:** | | |
| *A-1 Sauce* | 1 tsp. | 82 |
| Beef, chopped (patty only): | | |
| Regular | 3½ oz. | 58 |
| Double Deluxe | 5.9 oz. | 99 |
| Junior (*Square Shooter*) | 1.6 oz. | 27 |
| Steakhouse Deluxe | 2.96 oz. | 50 |
| Beverages: | | |
| *Coca-Cola* | 8 fl. oz. | 1 |

| Food and Description | Measure or Quantity | Sodium (mgs.) |
|---|---|---|
| Coffee | 6 fl. oz. | 26 |
| *Dr. Pepper* | 8 fl. oz. | 18 |
| Milk, chocolate | 8 fl. oz. | 149 |
| Orange drink | 8 fl. oz. | 12 |
| Root beer | 8 fl. oz. | 18 |
| *Sprite* | 8 fl. oz. | 31 |
| *Tab* | 8 fl. oz. | 18 |
| Bun: | | |
| Regular | 2.4-oz. bun | 334 |
| Hot dog | 1 bun | 263 |
| Junior | 1.4-oz. bun | 197 |
| Steakhouse deluxe | 2.4-oz. bun | 334 |
| Chicken strips: | | |
| Adult portion | 2¾ oz. | 420 |
| Child | 1.4 oz. | 210 |
| Cocktail sauce | 1½ oz. | 143 |
| Filet Mignon | 3.8 oz. (edible portion) | 82 |
| Filet of sole, fish only (See also Bun) | 3-oz, piece | 46 |
| Fish, baked | 4.9-oz. serving | 363 |
| Gelatin dessert | ½ cup | 55 |
| Gravy, au jus | 1 oz. | 125 |
| Ham & cheese: | | |
| Bun (See Bun) | | |
| Cheese, Swiss | 2 slices (.8 oz.) | 310 |
| Ham | 2½ oz. | 724 |
| Hot dog, child's, meat only (See also Bun) | 1.6-oz. hot dog | 542 |
| Margarine: | | |
| Pat | 1 tsp. | 49 |
| On potato, as served | ½ oz. | 138 |
| New York strip steak | 6.1 oz. (edible portion) | 79 |
| Onion, chopped | 1 T. | 1 |
| Pickle, dill | 3 slices (.7 oz.) | 279 |
| Potato: | | |
| Baked | 7.2-oz. potato | 6 |
| French fries | 3-oz. serving | 5 |
| Prime ribs: | | |
| Regular | 4.2 oz. (edible portion) | 71 |
| Imperial | 8.4 oz. (edible portion) | 141 |
| King | 6 oz. (edible portion) | 101 |
| Pudding, chocolate | 4½ oz. | 177 |

| Food and Description | Measure or Quantity | Sodium (mgs.) |
|---|---|---|
| Ribeye | 3.2 oz. (edible portion) | 271 |
| Ribeye & Shrimp: | | |
| Ribeye | 3.2 oz. | 271 |
| Shrimp | 2.2 oz. | 114 |
| Roll, kaiser | 2.2-oz. roll | 311 |
| Salad bar: | | |
| Beets | 1 oz. | 56 |
| Broccoli | 1 oz. | 4 |
| Cabbage, red | 1 oz. | 7 |
| Carrots | 1 oz. | 13 |
| Cauliflower | 1 oz. | 4 |
| Celery | 1 oz. | 36 |
| Chickpeas (Garbanzos) | 1 oz. | 7 |
| Cucumber | 1 oz. | 2 |
| Mushrooms | 1 oz. | 4 |
| Onion, white | 1 oz. | 3 |
| Pepper, green | 1 oz. | 4 |
| Radish | 1 oz. | 5 |
| Tomato | 1 oz. | Tr. |
| Salad dressing: | | |
| Blue cheese | 1 oz. | 265 |
| Italian, creamy | 1 oz. | 419 |
| Low calorie | 1 oz. | 220 |
| Oil & vinegar | 1 oz. | Tr. |
| Thousand Island | 1 oz. | 170 |
| Shrimp dinner | 7 pieces (3½ oz.) | 182 |
| Sirloin: | | |
| Regular | 3.3 oz. (edible portion) | 372 |
| Super | 6½ oz. (edible portion) | 695 |
| Tips | 4 oz. (edible portion) | 375 |
| Steak sauce | 1 oz. | 329 |
| Tartar sauce | 1.5 oz. | 300 |
| T-Bone | 4.3 oz. (edible portion) | 545 |
| Tomato (See also Salad Bar): | | |
| Slices | 2 slices (.9 oz.) | 7 |
| Whole, small | 3.5 oz. | 3 |
| Topping, whipped | ¼ oz. | 4 |
| **POPCORN:** | | |
| *Plain, popped fresh: | | |
| (Jiffy Pop) buttered, with salt | ½ of 5-oz. pkg. | 936 |
| (Pillsbury) Microwave Popcorn: | | |
| Regular | 1 cup | 129 |

| Food and Description | Measure or Quantity | Sodium (mgs.) |
|---|---|---|
| Butter flavor | 1 cup | 176 |
| (Super Pop) dry popped, white or yellow | 1 oz. | Tr. |
| Packaged (Tom's): | | |
| Regular | 1 oz. | 300 |
| Cheese | 1 oz. | 460 |
| *POPOVER MIX (Flako) | 1 popover | 355 |
| POPPY SEED (French's) | 1 tsp. | Tr. |
| POP TARTS (See TOASTER CAKE OR PASTRY) | | |
| PORGY, meat only, raw | 4 oz. | 71 |
| PORK: | | |
| Fresh: | | |
| Chop: | | |
| Broiled, lean & fat | 3-oz. chop (weighed without bone) | 55 |
| Broiled, lean only | 3-oz. chop (weighed without bone) | 55 |
| Loin: | | |
| Roasted, lean & fat | 4 oz. | 74 |
| Roasted, lean only | 4 oz. | 74 |
| Cured ham, roasted, lean only | 4 oz. | 1055 |
| PORK DINNER, frozen (Swanson) 4-compartment | 11¼-oz. dinner | 635 |
| PORK, PACKAGED (Eckrich) | 1 oz. | 350 |
| PORK RINDS, (Tom's), regular | 1-oz. serving | 220 |
| PORT WINE: | | |
| (Gold Seal) | 3 fl. oz. | 3 |
| (Great Western) | 3 fl. oz. | 34 |
| *POSTUM, instant | 6 fl. oz. | 3 |
| POTATO: | | |
| Cooked: | | |
| Au gratin | ½ cup | 433 |
| Baked, peeled | 2½" dia. potato | 4 |
| Boiled, peeled | 4.2-oz. potato | 2 |
| French-fried | 10 pieces | 3 |
| Hash-browned, home recipe | ½ cup | 281 |
| Mashed, milk & butter added | ½ cup | 324 |
| Canned, solids & liq.: | | |
| (Del Monte) | ½ cup | 355 |
| (Sunshine) | 1 cup | 753 |
| Frozen: | | |
| (Birds Eye): | | |
| Cottage fries | 2.8-oz. serving | 14 |
| Crinkle cuts, regular | 3-oz. serving | 36 |
| Farm style wedge | 3-oz. serving | 25 |
| French fries, regular | 3-oz. serving | 23 |

| Food and Description | Measure or Quantity | Sodium (mgs.) |
|---|---|---|
| Hash browns, shredded | ¼ of 12-oz. pkg. | 21 |
| *Tasti Puffs* | ¼ of 10-oz. pkg. | 401 |
| *Tiny Taters* | ⅓ of 16-oz. pkg. | 282 |
| Whole peeled | 3.2 oz. | 5 |
| (Green Giant): | | |
| Sliced, in butter sauce | ½ cup | 470 |
| & sweet peas in bacon cream sauce | ½ cup | 400 |
| (McKenzie) whole, white | 3.2 oz. | 5 |
| (Stouffer's): | | |
| Au gratin | ⅓ pkg. | 480 |
| Scalloped | ⅓ pkg. | 450 |
| **POTATO & BACON,** canned | | |
| (Hormel) *Short Orders,* au gratin | 7½-oz. can | 942 |
| **POTATO CHIP:** | | |
| (Featherweight) unsalted | 1 oz. | 6 |
| (Frito-Lay's) natural | 1 oz. | 265 |
| (Laura Scudder's): | | |
| Barbecue | 1 oz. | 200 |
| Sour cream & onion | 1 oz. | 170 |
| *Lay's,* sour cream & onion flavor | 1 oz. | 407 |
| *Pringle's:* | | |
| Regular | 1 oz. | 216 |
| *Cheez-Ums* | 1 oz. | 240 |
| Light | 1 oz. | 152 |
| Rippled | 1 oz. | 250 |
| (Tom's): | | |
| Regular | 1 oz. | 200 |
| BBQ | 1 oz. | 280 |
| Hot | 1 oz. | 310 |
| Vinegar & salt | 1 oz. | 280 |
| **POTATO & HAM,** canned (Hormel) *Short Orders,* scalloped | 7½-oz. serving | 1189 |
| **\*POTATO MIX:** | | |
| Au gratin: | | |
| (Betty Crocker) | ½ cup | 605 |
| (French's) *Big Tate,* tangy | ½ cup | 525 |
| Creamed (Betty Crocker) | ½ cup | 385 |
| Hash browns (Betty Crocker) with onion | ½ cup | 460 |
| Hickory smoke cheese (Betty Crocker) | ½ cup | 650 |
| Julienne (Betty Crocker) with mild cheese sauce | ½ cup | 570 |
| Mashed: | | |
| (American Beauty) | ½ cup | 340 |
| (Betty Crocker) *Buds* | ½ cup | 355 |

| Food and Description | Measure or Quantity | Sodium (mgs.) |
|---|---|---|
| (Pillsbury) *Hungry Jack*, flakes | ½ cup | 410 |
| Scalloped: | | |
| (Betty Crocker) | ½ cup | 570 |
| (French's) *Big Tate* | ½ cup | 540 |
| Sour cream & chive (Betty Crocker) | ½ cup | 495 |
| **\*POTATO PANCAKE MIX** | | |
| (French's) *Big Tate* | 3″ pancake | 163 |
| **POTATO SALAD**, home recipe | ½ cup | 600 |
| **POTATO STICKS** (Durkee) *O & C* | 1½-oz. can | 383 |
| **POTATO, STUFFED, BAKED,** frozen (Green Giant): | | |
| With cheese flavored topping | ½ of 10-oz. pkg | 520 |
| With sour cream & chives | ½ of 10-oz. pkg. | 580 |
| **POUND CAKE** (See CAKE, Pound) | | |
| **PRESERVES OR JAM** (See individual flavors) | | |
| **PRETZEL:** | | |
| (Estee) unsalted | 1 piece | Tr. |
| (Featherweight) unsalted | 1 piece | Tr. |
| (Pepperidge Farm): | | |
| Nuggets | 1¼-oz. serving | 497 |
| Sticks, thin | 1¼-oz. serving | 492 |
| (Tom's) twists | 1 oz. | 430 |
| **PRODUCT 19,** cereal (Kellogg's) | 1 cup | 290 |
| **PRUNE:** | | |
| Canned: | | |
| (Featherweight) stewed, water pack | ½ cup | <10 |
| (Sunsweet) stewed | ½ cup | 2 |
| Dried: | | |
| (Del Monte) Moist Pak | 2 oz. | <10 |
| (Sunsweet) whole or pitted | 2 oz. | 3 |
| **PRUNE JUICE:** | | |
| (Del Monte) | 6 fl. oz. | 4 |
| (Sunsweet): | | |
| Regular | 6 fl. oz. | 4 |
| With pulp | 6 fl. oz. | 12 |
| **PUDDING OR PIE FILLING:** | | |
| Canned, regular pack: | | |
| Banana (Del Monte) | | |
| *Pudding Cup* | 5-oz. container | 277 |
| Butterscotch (Del Monte) | | |
| *Pudding Cup* | 5-oz. container | 277 |
| Chocolate: | | |
| (Betty Crocker) | 5-oz. container | 260 |
| (Del Monte) *Pudding Cup* | 5-oz. container | 327 |
| Rice (Comstock; Menner's) | ½ of 7½-oz. can | 450 |

| Food and Description | Measure or Quantity | Sodium (mgs.) |
|---|---|---|
| Tapioca: | | |
| (Betty Crocker) | 4¼-oz. container | 170 |
| (Del Monte) *Pudding Cup* | 5-oz. container | 253 |
| (Hunt's) *Snack Pack* | 5-oz. container | 210 |
| Vanilla (Del Monte) | 5-oz. container | 320 |
| Chilled, *Swiss Miss:* | | |
| Butterscotch, chocolate or chocolate malt | 4-oz. container | 175 |
| Double rich | 4-oz. container | 173 |
| Rice | 4-oz. container | 295 |
| Tapioca | 4-oz. container | 170 |
| Frozen (Rich's): | | |
| Banana | 3-oz. container | 118 |
| Butterscotch or vanilla | 4½-oz. container | 192 |
| Chocolate | 4½-oz. container | 205 |
| Vanilla | 4½-oz. container | 243 |
| *Mix, sweetened, regular & instant: | | |
| Banana: | | |
| (Jell-O) cream, regular | ½ cup | 257 |
| (Royal) regular | ½ cup | 229 |
| Butter pecan (Jell-O) instant | ½ cup | 442 |
| Butterscotch: | | |
| (Jell-O) instant | ½ cup | 483 |
| (Royal) | ½ cup | 229 |
| Chocolate: | | |
| (Jell-O) regular | ½ cup | 170 |
| (My-T-Fine) regular | ½ cup | 171 |
| Coconut: | | |
| (Jell-O) cream, regular | ½ cup | 216 |
| (Royal) instant | ½ cup | 323 |
| Custard (Royal) regular | ½ cup | 131 |
| Flan (Royal) regular | ½ cup | 131 |
| Lemon: | | |
| (Jell-O) instant | ½ cup | 397 |
| (Royal) regular | ½ cup | 94 |
| Lime (Royal) Key Lime, regular | ½ cup | 94 |
| Pineapple (Jell-O) cream, regular | ½ cup | 400 |
| Pistachio (Jell-O) instant | ½ cup | 445 |
| Raspberry (Salada) *Danish Dessert* | ½ cup | 5 |
| Rice, *Jell-O Americana* | ½ cup | 158 |
| Strawberry (Salada) *Danish Desserts* | ½ cup | 5 |
| Tapioca: | | |
| *Jell-O Americana*, chocolate or vanilla | ½ cup | 170 |
| (Royal) chocolate | ½ cup | 140 |

| Food and Description | Measure or Quantity | Sodium (mgs.) |
|---|---|---|
| Vanilla: | | |
| (Jell-O) French, regular | ½ cup | 201 |
| (Royal) | ½ cup | 229 |
| *Mix, dietetic: | | |
| Butterscotch: | | |
| (Dia-Mel) | ½ cup | 80 |
| (D-Zerta) | ½ cup | 115 |
| (Estee) | ½ cup | 80 |
| (Featherweight) artificially sweetened | ½ cup | 70 |
| Chocolate: | | |
| (Dia-Mel) | ½ cup | 80 |
| (D-Zerta) | ½ cup | 116 |
| (Estee) | ½ cup | 75 |
| Lemon: | | |
| (Dia-Mel) | ½ cup | 20 |
| (Estee) | ½ cup | 75 |
| Vanilla: | | |
| (Dia-Mel) | ½ cup | 80 |
| (D-Zerta) | ½ cup | 105 |
| (Estee) | ½ cup | 75 |
| (Featherweight) artificially sweetened | ½ cup | 70 |
| **PUDDING STIX** (Good Humor) | 1¾-oz. pop | 65 |
| **PUFFED RICE:** | | |
| (Malt-O-Meal) | 1 cup | 1 |
| (Quaker) | 1 cup | 1 |
| **PUFFED WHEAT:** | | |
| (Malt-O-Meal) | 1 cup | 1 |
| (Quaker) | 1 cup | 1 |
| **PUMPKIN,** canned (Libby's) solid pack | ½ cup | 10 |

# Q

| Food and Description | Measure or Quantity | Sodium (mgs.) |
|---|---|---|
| **QUAIL**, raw, meat & skin | 4 oz. | 45 |
| *QUIK* (Nestlé): | | |
| Chocolate | 1 tsp. | 18 |
| Strawberry | 1 tsp. | 10 |
| *QUISP*, cereal | 1⅙ cup | 189 |

# R

| Food and Description | Measure or Quantity | Sodium (mgs.) |
|---|---|---|
| **RADISH** | 2 small radishes | 4 |
| **RAISIN,** dried: | | |
| (Del Monte) golden | 3 oz. | 15 |
| (Sun-Maid) | 3 oz. | 12 |
| ***RAISINS, RICE & RYE,*** cereal | | |
| (Kellogg's) | ¾ cup | 235 |
| ***RALSTON,*** cereal | ¼ cup | 3 |
| **RASPBERRY**: | | |
| Fresh: | | |
| Black, trimmed | ½ cup | Tr. |
| Red, trimmed | ½ cup | Tr. |
| Frozen (Birds Eye) quick thaw | 5-oz. serving | 1 |
| **RASPBERRY PRESERVE OR JAM:** | | |
| Sweetened (Smucker's) | 1 T. | 2 |
| Dietetic: | | |
| (Dia-Mel) | 1 T. | <3 |
| (Louis Sherry) | 1 T. | <3 |
| **RATATOUILLE,** frozen (Stouffer's) | 5-oz. serving | 1320 |
| **RAVIOLI:** | | |
| Canned, regular pack (Franco-American): | | |
| Beef, in meat sauce | 7½-oz. can | 1095 |
| Beef, *RavioliOs* | 7½-oz. serving | 1030 |
| Cheese, in tomato sauce, *RavioliOs* | 7½-oz. can | 1160 |
| Canned, dietetic (Featherweight) beef | 8-oz. can | 68 |
| **RELISH:** | | |
| Dill (Vlasic) | 1 oz. | 422 |
| Hamburger (Vlasic) | 1 oz. | 260 |
| Hot dog (Vlasic) | 1 oz. | 260 |
| Sweet: | | |
| (Smucker's) | 1 T. | 158 |
| (Vlasic) | 1 oz. | 224 |

| Food and Description | Measure or Quantity | Sodium (mgs.) |
|---|---|---|
| **RENNET MIX** (Junket): | | |
| *Powder, any flavor: | | |
| Made with skim milk | ½ cup | 70 |
| Made with whole milk | ½ cup | 65 |
| Tablet | 1 tablet | 165 |
| **RHINE WINE:** | | |
| (Gold Seal) | 3 fl. oz. | 3 |
| (Great Western) | 3 fl. oz. | 25 |
| **RHUBARB,** cooked, sweetened | ½ cup | 2 |
| ***RICE:** | | |
| Brown (Uncle Ben's) parboiled, with added butter & salt | ⅔ cup | 458 |
| White (Minute Rice) instant, no added butter or salt | ⅔ cup | 2 |
| **RICE, FRIED** (See also RICE MIX): | | |
| *Canned (La Choy) | ⅓ of 11-oz. can | 965 |
| Frozen: | | |
| (Birds Eye) | 3.7-oz. serving | 432 |
| (Green Giant) | 10-oz. entree | 1130 |
| (La Choy) & pork | 8-oz. serving | 1770 |
| **RICE, FRIED, SEASONING MIX** | | |
| (Kikkoman) | 1-oz. pkg. | 2 |
| **RICE KRINKLES,** CEREAL (Post) | ⅞ cup | 179 |
| **RICE KRISPIES,** cereal (Kellogg's): | | |
| Regular | 1 cup | 285 |
| Frosted | ¾ cup | 200 |
| ***RICE MIX:** | | |
| Beef: | | |
| (Lipton) | ½ cup | 665 |
| (Minute Rice) | ½ cup | 694 |
| Chicken: | | |
| (Lipton) & sauce | ½ cup | 525 |
| (Minute Rice) | ½ cup | 694 |
| Herb & butter (Lipton) & sauce | ½ cup | 500 |
| Long grain & wild (Minute Rice) | ½ cup | 578 |
| Medley (Lipton) | ½ cup | 400 |
| Mushroom (Lipton) & sauce | ½ cup | 560 |
| Spanish (Minute Rice) | ½ cup | 839 |
| **RICE, SPANISH:** | | |
| Canned: | | |
| Regular pack (Comstock; Menner's) | ½ of 7½-oz. can | 850 |
| Dietetic (Featherweight) low sodium | 7½-oz. serving | 32 |
| Frozen (Birds Eye) | 3.7-oz. serving | 495 |
| **RICE & VEGETABLE,** frozen: | | |
| (Birds Eye): | | |
| French style | 3.7-oz. serving | 637 |
| & peas with mushrooms | 2⅓ oz. | 322 |

| Food and Description | Measure or Quantity | Sodium (mgs.) |
|---|---|---|
| (Green Giant) *Rice Originals:* | | |
|   & broccoli in cheese sauce | | |
|     or festive | ½ cup | 405 |
|   With herb butter sauce | ½ cup | 420 |
|   Long grain & white | ½ cup | 565 |
|   Pilaf | ½ cup | 520 |
| **ROE,** baked or broiled, cod & shad | 4 oz. | 83 |
| **ROLL OR BUN:** | | |
|   Commercial type, non-frozen: | | |
|     Biscuit (Wonder) | 1-oz. piece | 140 |
|     Brown & serve (Wonder) | | |
|       *Gem Style* | 1-oz. piece | 140 |
|     Crescent (Pepperidge Farm) | | |
|       butter | 1-oz. piece | 165 |
|     Croissant (Pepperidge Farm): | | |
|       Almond | 2-oz. piece | 260 |
|       Butter | 2-oz. piece | 310 |
|       Chocolate | 2.4-oz. piece | 325 |
|       Cinnamon | 2-oz. piece | 280 |
|       Walnut | 2-oz. piece | 275 |
|     Dinner: | | |
|       *Home Pride* | 1-oz. piece | 170 |
|       (Pepperidge Farm) | .7-oz. piece | 95 |
|       (Wonder) | 1-oz. piece | 140 |
|     Finger (Pepperidge Farm) | | |
|       sesame seed | .6-oz. piece | 120 |
|     Frankfurter: | | |
|       (Arnold) Hot Dog | 1.3-oz. piece | 290 |
|       (Pepperidge Farm) | 1¾-oz. piece | 240 |
|       (Wonder) | 1-oz. piece | 150 |
|     French: | | |
|       (Arnold) *Francisco,* sourdough | 1.1-oz. piece | 160 |
|       (Pepperidge Farm): | | |
|         Small | 1.3-oz. piece | 245 |
|         Large | 3-oz. piece | 550 |
|     *Golden Twist* (Pepperidge Farm) | 1-oz. piece | 150 |
|     Hamburger: | | |
|       (Arnold) | 1.4-oz. piece | 285 |
|       (Pepperidge Farm) | 1.5-oz. piece | 250 |
|       (Wonder) | 1-oz. piece | 150 |
|     Hoggie (Wonder) | 5-oz. piece | 840 |
|     Honey (Hostess) glazed | 3.75-oz. piece | 650 |
|     Old fashioned (Pepperidge Farm) | .6-oz. piece | 95 |
|     Pan (Wonder) | 1¼-oz. piece | 188 |
|     Parkerhouse (Pepperidge Farm) | .6-oz. piece | 95 |
|     Party (Pepperidge Farm) | .4-oz. piece | 55 |
|     Sandwich (Arnold) soft, plain | 1.3-oz. piece | 260 |

| Food and Description | Measure or Quantity | Sodium (mgs.) |
|---|---|---|
| Soft (Pepperidge Farm) | 1¼-oz. piece | 235 |
| Sourdough, french (Pepperidge Farm) | 1.3-oz. piece | 255 |
| Frozen: | | |
| Apple crunch (Sara Lee) | 1-oz. piece | 105 |
| Caramel pecan (Sara Lee) | 1.3-oz. piece | 148 |
| Caramel sticky (Sara Lee) | 1.03-oz. piece | 110 |
| Cinnamon (Sara Lee) | .9-oz. piece | 96 |
| Croissant (Sara Lee) | .9-oz. piece | 140 |
| Crumb (Sara Lee) French | 1¾-oz. piece | 170 |
| Danish (Sara Lee): | | |
| Apple | 1.3-oz. piece | 110 |
| Cheese | 1.3-oz. piece | 124 |
| Cinnamon raisin | 1.3-oz. piece | 132 |
| Pecan | 1.3-oz. piece | 119 |
| Honey (Morton) mini | 1.3-oz. piece | 90 |
| *ROLL OR BUN DOUGH: | | |
| Frozen (Rich's): | | |
| Cinnamon | 2¼-oz. piece | 226 |
| Frankfurter | 1 piece | 238 |
| Hamburger, regular | 1 piece | 227 |
| Parkerhouse | 1 piece | 133 |
| Refrigerated (Pillsbury): | | |
| Apple danish, *Pipin' Hot* | 1 piece | 250 |
| Caramel danish, with nuts | 1 piece | 245 |
| Cinnamon raisin danish | 1 piece | 225 |
| Crescent | 1 piece | 230 |
| Orange danish with icing | 1 piece | 242 |
| White, bakery style | 1 piece | 350 |
| *ROLL MIX, HOT (Pillsbury) | 1 piece | 125 |
| *ROMAN MEAL CEREAL:* | | |
| 2- or 5-minute | ⅓ cup | 2 |
| 5-minute, with oats | ⅓ cup | 6 |
| ROSEMARY LEAVES (French's) | 1 tsp. | Tr. |
| ROSE WINE (Great Western) | 3 fl. oz. | 38 |
| *ROY ROGERS:* | | |
| Bar Burger, R.R. | 1 burger | 1820 |
| Biscuit | 1 biscuit | 575 |
| Breakfast crescent sandwich: | | |
| Regular | 4.5-oz. sandwich | 867 |
| With bacon | 4.7-oz. sandwich | 1035 |
| With ham | 5.8-oz. sandwich | 1192 |
| With sausage | 5.7-oz. sandwich | 1289 |
| Brownie | 1 piece | 150 |
| Cheeseburger: | | |
| Regular | 1 burger | 601 |

| Food and Description | Measure or Quantity | Sodium (mgs.) |
|---|---|---|
| With bacon | 1 burger | 1535 |
| Chicken: | | |
| Breast | 1 piece | 601 |
| Leg | 1 piece | 162 |
| Thigh | 1 piece | 505 |
| Wing | 1 piece | 266 |
| Cole slaw | 3½-oz. serving | 261 |
| Danish: | | |
| Apple | 1 piece | 255 |
| Cheese | 1 piece | 260 |
| Cherry | 1 piece | 242 |
| Drinks: | | |
| Coffee, black | 6 fl. oz. | 2 |
| Coke: | | |
| Regular | 12 fl. oz. | 22 |
| Diet | 12 fl. oz. | 52 |
| Hot chocolate | 6 fl. oz. | 124 |
| Milk | 8 fl. oz. | 110 |
| Orange juice: | | |
| Regular | 7 fl. oz. | 2 |
| Large | 10 fl. oz. | 3 |
| Shake: | | |
| Chocolate | 1 shake | 290 |
| Vanilla | 1 shake | 261 |
| Strawberry | 1 shake | 282 |
| Tea, iced, plain | 8 fl. oz. | Tr. |
| Egg & biscuit platter: | | |
| Regular | 1 meal | 734 |
| With bacon | 1 meal | 957 |
| With ham | 1 meal | 1156 |
| With sausage | 1 meal | 1059 |
| Hamburger | 1 burger | 495 |
| Pancake platter, with syrup & butter: | | |
| Plain | 1 order | 842 |
| With bacon | 1 order | 1065 |
| With ham | 1 order | 1264 |
| With sausage | 1 order | 1167 |
| Potato: | | |
| Baked, *Hot Topped*: | | |
| Plain | 1 potato | 65 |
| With bacon & cheese | 1 potato | 778 |
| With broccoli & cheese | 1 potato | 523 |
| With margarine | 1 potato | 161 |
| With sour cream & chives | 1 potato | 138 |
| With taco beef & cheese | 1 potato | 726 |
| French fries: | | |
| Regular | 3 oz. | 165 |

| Food and Description | Measure or Quantity | Sodium (mgs.) |
|---|---|---|
| Large | 4 oz. | 220 |
| Potato salad | 3½-oz. order | 696 |
| Roast beef sandwich: | | |
| Plain: | | |
| Regular | 1 sandwich | 785 |
| Large | 1 sandwich | 1044 |
| With cheese: | | |
| Regular | 1 sandwich | 1694 |
| Large | 1 sandwich | 1953 |
| Salad bar: | | |
| Bacon bits | 1 T. | 210 |
| Beets, sliced | ¼ cup | 100 |
| Broccoli | ½ cup | 7 |
| Carrot, shredded | ¼ cup | 7 |
| Cheese, cheddar | ¼ cup | 7 |
| Croutons | 1 T. | 226 |
| Cucumber | 1 slice | Tr. |
| Egg, chopped | 1 T. | 21 |
| Lettuce | 1 cup | 7 |
| Macaroni salad | 1 T. | 155 |
| Mushrooms | ¼ cup | 3 |
| Noodle, Chinese | ¼ cup | 100 |
| Pea, green | ¼ cup | 66 |
| Pepper, green | 1 T. | 1 |
| Potato salad | 1 T. | 175 |
| Sunflower seeds | 1 T. | 3 |
| Tomato | 1 slice | 1 |
| Salad dressing: | | |
| Regular: | | |
| Bacon & tomato | 1 T. | 75 |
| Bleu cheese | 1 T. | 76 |
| Ranch | 1 T. | 50 |
| 1,000 Island | 1 T. | 75 |
| Low calorie, Italian | 1 T. | 50 |
| Strawberry shortcake | 7.2-oz. serving | 674 |
| Sundae: | | |
| Caramel | 1 sundae | 193 |
| Hot fudge | 1 sundae | 230 |
| Strawberry | 1 sundae | 99 |
| **RUTABAGA,** canned (Sunshine) solids & liq. | ½ cup | 393 |

# S

| Food and Description | Measure or Quantity | Sodium (mgs.) |
|---|---|---|
| **SAGE** (French's) | 1 tsp. | Tr. |
| **SALAD DRESSING:** | | |
| Regular: | | |
| Bleu or blue cheese | | |
| (Wish-Bone) chunky | 1 T. | 150 |
| Caesar (Wish-Bone) | 1 T. | 250 |
| Cheddar-bacon (Wish-Bone) | 1 T. | 110 |
| French: | | |
| Home recipe | 1 T. | 105 |
| (Bernstein's) creamy | 1 T. | 224 |
| (Wish-Bone) herbal | 1 T. | 130 |
| Italian: | | |
| (Bernstein's) | 1 T. | 184 |
| (Wish-Bone) Robusto | 1 T. | 285 |
| Russian (Wish-Bone) | 1 T. | 140 |
| Sour cream & bacon (Wish-Bone) | 1 T. | 95 |
| *Spin Blend* (Hellmann's) | 1 T. | 112 |
| Thousand Island (Bernstein's) | 1 T. | 127 |
| Dietetic or low calorie: | | |
| Bacon & Tomato (Wish-Bone) | 1 T. | 0 |
| Bleu or blue cheese: | | |
| (Dia-Mel) | 1 T. | 20 |
| (Walden Farms) chunky | 1 T. | 270 |
| Buttermilk (Wish-Bone) | 1 T. | 150 |
| Caesar: | | |
| (Estee) garlic | 1 T. | 150 |
| (Featherweight) creamy | 1 T. | 16 |
| Cucumber (Featherweight) creamy | 1 T. | 12 |
| Cucumber & onion: | | |
| (Dia-Mel) | 1 T. | 30 |
| (Featherweight) creamy | 1 T. | 12 |
| French: | | |
| (Dia-Mel) | 1 T. | 10 |
| (Featherweight) low calorie | 1 T. | 163 |
| (Walden Farms) chunky | 1 T. | 132 |

| Food and Description | Measure or Quantity | Sodium (mgs.) |
|---|---|---|
| Garlic (Dia-Mel) creamy | 1 T. | 10 |
| Herb & spice (Featherweight) | 1 T. | 5 |
| Italian: | | |
|   (Dia-Mel) | 1 T. | 10 |
|   (Estee) spicy | 1 T. | 150 |
|   (Featherweight) | 1 T. | 127 |
|   (Walden Farms) low sodium | 1 T. | 5 |
|   (Wish-Bone) regular | 1 T. | 210 |
| Onion & cucumber (Estee) | 1 T. | 80 |
| Red wine/vinegar (Featherweight) | 1 T. | 63 |
| Russian (Featherweight) creamy | 1 T. | 134 |
| Tahiti (Dia-Mel) | 1 T. | 5 |
| Thousand Island: | | |
|   (Dia-Mel) | 1 T. | 30 |
|   (Walden Farms) | 1 T. | 132 |
| 2-Calorie Low Sodium | | |
|   (Featherweight) | 1 T. | 6 |
| Whipped (Dia-Mel) *Tasti Diet* | 1 T. | 100 |
| Yogurt buttermilk (Dia-Mel) | 1 T. | 10 |
| **SALAD DRESSING MIX:** | | |
| *Regular (Good Seasons): | | |
| Blue cheese | 1 T. | 216 |
| Buttermilk, farm style | 1 T. | 137 |
| Farm style | 1 T. | 124 |
| French, old fashioned | 1 T. | 185 |
| Garlic, cheese | 1 T. | 173 |
| Garlic & herbs | 1 T. | 187 |
| Italian, regular | 1 T. | 172 |
| Tomato & herbs | 1 T. | 87 |
| Dietetic: | | |
| *Blue cheese (Weight Watchers) | 1 T. | 108 |
| *French (Weight Watchers) | 1 T. | 164 |
| *Italian: | | |
|   (Good Seasons) regular | 1 T. | 177 |
|   (Weight Watchers): | | |
|     Regular | 1 T. | 175 |
|     Creamy | 1 T. | 224 |
| *Russian (Weight Watchers) | 1 T. | 128 |
| *Thousand Island | | |
|   (Weight Watchers) | 1 T. | 265 |
| **SALAD LIFT** (French's) | 1 tsp. | 640 |
| **SALAMI:** | | |
| (Eckrich) hard | 1 oz. | 600 |
| (Hormel): | | |
| Beef | 1 slice | 110 |
| Genoa, packaged, sliced | 1 slice | 456 |
| Hard, National Brand | 1-oz. serving | 463 |

| Food and Description | Measure or Quantity | Sodium (mgs.) |
|---|---|---|
| (Oscar Mayer): | | |
| For beer, beef | .8-oz. slice | 233 |
| Cotto | .8-oz. slice | 245 |
| Hard | .3-oz. slice | 167 |
| (Swift) Genoa | 1-oz. serving | 642 |
| **SALISBURY STEAK,** frozen: | | |
| (Banquet): | | |
| *Buffet Supper* | 2-lb. pkg. | 4464 |
| *Cookin' Bag* | 5-oz. pkg. | 729 |
| Extra Helping | 19-oz. dinner | 2175 |
| (Green Giant) with gravy, | | |
| oven bake | ½ of entree | 1095 |
| (Morton) King Size | 19-oz. dinner | 2717 |
| (Stouffer's) *Lean Cuisine* | 9½-oz. pkg. | 820 |
| (Swanson): | | |
| Regular | 11-oz. dinner | 1055 |
| *Hungry Man* | 16½-oz. dinner | 1565 |
| **SALMON,** canned: | | |
| Regular pack, solids & liq.: | | |
| Keta (Bumble Bee) | ½ cup | 536 |
| Pink or Humpback: | | |
| (Bumble Bee) | ½ cup | 542 |
| (Del Monte) | 7¾-oz. can | 1220 |
| Sockeye or Red or Blueback: | | |
| (Bumble Bee) | ½ cup | 455 |
| (Del Monte) | 7¾-oz. can | 1169 |
| Canned, dietetic (S&W) *Nutradiet,* | | |
| low sodium | ½ cup | 45 |
| **SALT:** | | |
| Table: | | |
| (USDA) | 1 tsp. | 2132 |
| Regular (Morton) | 1 tsp. | 2544 |
| *Lite* (Morton) | 1 tsp. | 1188 |
| Hickory smoke (French's) | 1 tsp. | 1170 |
| Substitute: | | |
| (Adolph's) plain | 1 tsp. | Tr. |
| (Dia-Mel) | 1 tsp. | 1 |
| (Morton) plain | 1 tsp. | Tr. |
| **SANDWICH SPREAD:** | | |
| (Hellmann's) | 1 T. | 191 |
| (Oscar Mayer) | 1-oz. serving | 279 |
| **SARDINE,** canned: | | |
| Atlantic (Del Monte) in | | |
| tomato sauce | 7½-oz. can | 827 |
| Imported (Underwood) in mustard | | |
| or tomato sauce | 3¾-oz. can | 850 |
| Norwegian (Underwood) in oil | 3-oz. can | 800 |

111

| Food and Description | Measure or Quantity | Sodium (mgs.) |
|---|---|---|
| **SAUCE:** | | |
| Regular: | | |
| *A-1* | 1 T. | 275 |
| Barbecue: | | |
| *Chris & Pitt's* | 1 T. | 141 |
| (French's) smoky | 1 T. | 295 |
| *Open Pit* (General Foods) original | 1 T. | 236 |
| Burrito (Del Monte) | ¼ cup | 355 |
| Chili (See CHILI SAUCE) | | |
| *Escoffier Sauce Diable* | 1 T. | 160 |
| *Escoffier Sauce Robert* | 1 T. | 70 |
| *Famous Sauce* | 1 T. | 67 |
| Hot, *Frank's* | 1 tsp. | 131 |
| Italian (See also SPAGHETTI SAUCE or TOMATO SAUCE) (Contadina) | 4-oz. serving | 601 |
| Salsa Mexicana (Contadina) | 4 fl. oz. | 570 |
| Salsa Picante (Del Monte) hot | ¼ cup | 385 |
| Salsa Roja (Del Monte) | ¼ cup | 510 |
| Seafood cocktail (Del Monte) | 1 T. | 228 |
| Soy: | | |
| (Kikkoman): | | |
| Regular | 1 T. | 932 |
| Lite | 1 T. | 603 |
| (La Choy) | 1 T. | 974 |
| Steak (Dawn Fresh) with mushrooms | 1-oz. serving | 150 |
| *Steak Supreme* | 1 T. | 125 |
| Sweet & so : | | |
| (Contadina) | 4 fl. oz. | 500 |
| (La Choy) | 1-oz. serving | 222 |
| Swiss steak (Carnatin) | 2-oz. serving | 319 |
| Tabasco | ¼ tsp. | 9 |
| Taco (Ortega) | 1 T. | 80 |
| Tartar (Hellmann's) | 1 T. | 182 |
| Teriyaki (Kikkoman) | 1 T. | 612 |
| *V-8* | 1-oz. serving | 270 |
| White, medium | ¼ cup | 243 |
| Worcestershire: | | |
| (French's) regular or smoky | 1 T. | 165 |
| (Lea & Perrins) | 1 T. | 175 |
| Dietetic (Estee): | | |
| Barbecue | 1 T. | 3 |
| Cocktail | 1 T. | 2 |
| **SAUCE MIX:** | | |
| Regular: | | |
| À la King (Durkee) | 1-oz. pkg. | 1384 |

| Food and Description | Measure or Quantity | Sodium (mgs.) |
|---|---|---|
| *Cheese: | | |
| (Durkee) | ½ cup | 446 |
| (French's) | ½ cup | 850 |
| Hollandaise: | | |
| (Durkee) | 1-oz. pkg. | 548 |
| *(French's) | 1 T. | 97 |
| *Sour cream (French's) | 2½ T. | 130 |
| *Stroganoff (French's) | ⅓ cup | 490 |
| *Sweet & sour (Durkee) | 1 cup | 1053 |
| *Teriyaki (French's) | 1 T. | 593 |
| *White (Durkee) | 1 cup | 696 |
| *Dietetic (Weight Watchers) lemon butter | 1 T. | 1895 |
| **SAUERKRAUT,** canned: | | |
| (Claussen) drained | ½ cup | 491 |
| (Comstock) regular, solids & liq. | ½ cup | 800 |
| (Del Monte) solids & liq. | ½ cup | 775 |
| (Silver Floss) solids & liq. | ½ cup | 750 |
| (Vlasic) | 1 oz. | 284 |
| **SAUSAGE:** | | |
| *Brown & serve (Hormel) original | 1 link | 215 |
| Patty (Hormel) | 1 patty | 549 |
| Polish-style: | | |
| (Eckrich) meat | 1-oz. serving | 260 |
| (Hormel) Kilbase | 3-oz. serving | 904 |
| Pork: | | |
| *(Hormel) *Little-Sizzlers* | 1 link | 96 |
| (Jimmy Dean) | 2-oz. serving | 338 |
| *(Oscar Mayer) *Little Friers* | .6-oz. link | 223 |
| Roll (Eckrich) minced | 1-oz. slice | 340 |
| Smoked: | | |
| (Eckrich): | | |
| Beef, *Smok-Y-Links* | .8-oz. link | 200 |
| Meat | 2-oz. serving | 530 |
| (Hormel) Smokies, cheese | 1 sausage | 311 |
| (Oscar Mayer) beef | 1½-oz. link | 455 |
| Vienna: | | |
| (Hormel) regular | 1 sausage | 120 |
| (Libby's) in beef broth | 1 link | 94 |
| **SAUTERNE:** | | |
| (Gold Seal) | 3 fl. oz. | 3 |
| (Great Western) | 3 fl. oz. | 34 |
| **SCALLOP:** | | |
| Steamed | 4-oz. serving | 301 |
| Frozen: | | |
| (Mrs. Paul's) breaded & fried | 3½-oz. serving | 545 |
| (Stouffer's) *Lean Cuisine* | 11-oz. pkg. | 1325 |

| Food and Description | Measure or Quantity | Sodium (mgs.) |
|---|---|---|
| **SCREWDRIVER COCKTAIL** | | |
| (Mr. Boston) 12½% alcohol | 3 fl. oz. | 104 |
| **SEAFOOD NEWBURG,** frozen | | |
| (Mrs. Paul's) | 8½-oz. entree | 610 |
| **SEAFOOD PLATTER,** frozen | | |
| (Mrs. Paul's) breaded & fried | 9-oz. serving | 1340 |
| *SEGO* **DIET FOOD,** canned: | | |
| Regular: | | |
| Very banana, very strawberry, or very vanilla | 10 fl. oz. | 360 |
| Very chocolate or dutch chocolate | 10 fl. oz. | 445 |
| Lite: | | |
| Chocolate, chocolate malt or dutch chocolate | 10 fl. oz. | 475 |
| French vanilla or vanilla | 10 fl. oz. | 390 |
| **SESAME SEEDS** (French's) | 1 tsp. | Tr. |
| **7-GRAIN CEREAL** (Loma Linda) | | |
| no sugar | 1 oz. | 75 |
| **SHAD, CREOLE** | 4-oz. serving | 83 |
| *SHAKE'N BAKE:* | | |
| Chicken, original | 1 pkg. | 2363 |
| Chicken, barbecue | 1 pkg. | 3280 |
| Crispy country mild | 1 pkg. | 2041 |
| Fish | 2-oz. pkg. | 1049 |
| Italian | 1 pkg. | 2098 |
| Pork, barbecue | 1 pkg. | 2644 |
| **SHELLS, PASTA, STUFFED,** frozen (Stouffer's): | | |
| Beef & spinach | 9-oz. serving | 1310 |
| Cheese | 9-oz. serving | 1060 |
| Chicken | 9-oz. serving | 1315 |
| **SHERBERT** (Baskin-Robbins): | | |
| Daiquiri Ice | 1 scoop (2½ fl. oz.) | 11 |
| Orange | 1 scoop (2½ fl. oz.) | 29 |
| **SHERRY:** | | |
| Cocktail (Gold Seal) | 3 fl. oz. | 3 |
| Cream (Great Western) Solera | 3 fl. oz. | 32 |
| **SHREDDED WHEAT** (Quaker) | 1 biscuit | Tr. |
| **SHRIMP:** | | |
| Raw, whole | 1 lb. (weighed in shell) | 438 |
| Frozen (Mrs. Paul's) fried, oriental | 11-oz. serving | 940 |
| **SHRIMP DINNER,** frozen: | | |
| (Stouffer's) Newburg | 6½-oz. serving | 555 |
| (Van de Kamp's) | 10-oz. dinner | 880 |

| Food and Description | Measure or Quantity | Sodium (mgs.) |
|---|---|---|
| **SLENDER** (Carnation): | | |
| Bar: | | |
| Chocolate or chocolate peanut butter | 1 bar | 142 |
| Chocolate chip | 1 bar | 157 |
| Dry, chocolate or french vanilla | 1 packet | 110 |
| Liquid: | | |
| Banana, peach or strawberry | 10-fl.-oz. can | 430 |
| Chocolate | 10-fl.-oz. can | 515 |
| Vanilla | 10-fl.-oz. can | 550 |
| **SLOPPY HOT DOG SEASONING MIX** (French's) | 1½-oz. pkg. | 220 |
| **SLOPPY JOE:** | | |
| Canned (Libby's) beef | ⅓ cup | 190 |
| Frozen (Banquet) *Cookin' Bag* | 5-oz. pkg. | 730 |
| **SLOPPY JOE SAUCE** (Ragú) | | |
| *Joe Sauce* | *3½ oz.* | *645* |
| **SLOPPY JOE SEASONING MIX:** | | |
| *(Durkee) pizza flavor | 1¼ cups | 1515 |
| (French's) | 1½-oz. pkg. | 3120 |
| **SMURF BERRY CRUNCH,** cereal (Post) | 1 cup | 65 |
| **SNACK BAR** (Pepperidge Farm): | | |
| Apple nut, apricot-raspberry, blueberry or date nut | 1.7-oz. piece | 90 |
| Brownie nut | 1½-oz. piece | 100 |
| Chocolate chip or raisin spice | 1½-oz. piece | 100 |
| **SNO BALL** (Hostess) | 1 piece | 170 |
| **SOFT DRINK** | | |
| Sweetened: | | |
| Birch beer (Canada Dry) | 6 fl. oz. | 14 |
| Bitter lemon: | | |
| (Canada Dry) | 6 fl. oz. | 13 |
| (Schweppes) | 6 fl. oz. | 2 |
| *Bubble Up* | 6 fl. oz. | 16 |
| *Cactus Cooler* (Canada Dry) | 6 fl. oz. | 16 |
| Cherry: | | |
| (Canada Dry) wild | 6 fl. oz. | 16 |
| (Shasta) black | 6 fl. oz. | 18 |
| Club (Canada Dry) | 6 fl. oz. | 39 |
| Cola: | | |
| *Coca-Cola:* | | |
| Regular | 6 fl. oz. | 7 |
| Caffeine-free | 6 fl. oz. | 3 |
| *Pepsi-Cola,* regular or *Pepsi Free* | 6 fl. oz. | 2 |
| *RC 100,* caffeine-free | 6 fl. oz. | Tr. |

| Food and Description | Measure or Quantity | Sodium (mgs.) |
|---|---|---|
| (Shasta) | 6 fl. oz. | 13 |
| Collins mix (Canada Dry) | 6 fl. oz. | 14 |
| Cream: | | |
| (Canada Dry) vanilla | 6 fl. oz. | 14 |
| (Schweppes) red | 6 fl. oz. | 15 |
| (Shasta) | 6 fl. oz. | 12 |
| *Dr. Pepper* | 6 fl. oz. | 9 |
| Fruit punch: | | |
| (Nehi) | 6 fl. oz. | 91 |
| (Shasta) | 6 fl. oz. | 15 |
| Ginger ale: | | |
| (Canada Dry) regular | 6 fl. oz. | 5 |
| (Fanta) | 6 fl. oz. | 14 |
| (Shasta) | 6 fl. oz. | 11 |
| Ginger beer (Schweppes) | 6 fl. oz. | 14 |
| Grape: | | |
| (Canada Dry) concord | 6 fl. oz. | 16 |
| (Fanta; Nehi) | 6 fl. oz. | 7 |
| (Hi-C) | 6 fl. oz. | 6 |
| (Schweppes) | 6 fl. oz. | 15 |
| Half & half (Canada Dry) | 6 fl. oz. | 13 |
| Hi-Spot (Canada Dry) | 6 fl. oz. | 19 |
| Lemon (Hi-C) | 6 fl. oz. | 6 |
| *Mello-Yello* | 6 fl. oz. | 14 |
| *Mountain Dew* | 6 fl. oz. | 16 |
| *Mr. PiBB* | 6 fl. oz. | 11 |
| Orange: | | |
| (Canada Dry) *Sunrise* | 6 fl. oz. | 16 |
| (Hi-C) | 6 fl. oz. | 7 |
| (Sunkist) | 6 fl. oz. | 21 |
| Peach (Nehi) | 6 fl. oz. | 16 |
| Pineapple (Canada Dry) | 6 fl. oz. | 16 |
| Quinine or tonic water | | |
| (Canada Dry; Schweppes) | 6 fl. oz. | 5 |
| Root beer: | | |
| *Barrelhead* (Canada Dry) | 6 fl. oz. | 13 |
| (Dad's) | 6 fl. oz. | 14 |
| *Rooti* (Canada Dry) | 6 fl. oz. | 13 |
| (Shasta) draft | 6 fl. oz. | 13 |
| *Seven-Up* | 6 fl. oz. | 10 |
| *Slice* | 6 fl. oz. | 2 |
| *Sprite* | 6 fl. oz. | 23 |
| Strawberry (Shasta) | 6 fl. oz. | 23 |
| *Tahitian Treat* (Canada Dry) | 6 fl. oz. | 16 |
| *Upper Ten* (Royal Crown) | 6 fl. oz. | 20 |
| *Wink* (Canada Dry) | 6 fl. oz. | 14 |

| Food and Description | Measure or Quantity | Sodium (mgs.) |
|---|---|---|
| Dietetic: | | |
| *Bubble Up*, sugar free | 6 fl. oz. | 48 |
| Cherry (Shasta) black | 6 fl. oz. | 24 |
| Chocolate (No-Cal) | 6 fl. oz. | 33 |
| Coffee (No-Cal) | 6 fl. oz. | 45 |
| Cola: | | |
| (Canada Dry); No-Cal) | 6 fl. oz. | 20 |
| *Coca Cola*, regular or | | |
| caffeine free | 6 fl. oz. | 13 |
| *Diet Rite* | 6 fl. oz. | <5 |
| *Pepsi, diet* | 6 fl. oz. | 2 |
| *RC 100* | 6 fl. oz. | 19 |
| Cream (Shasta) | 6 fl. oz. | 25 |
| *Dr. Pepper* | 6 fl. oz. | Tr. |
| *Fresca* | 6 fl. oz. | 18 |
| Ginger Ale: | | |
| (Canada Dry) | 6 fl. oz. | 22 |
| (No-Cal) | 6 fl. oz. | 30 |
| Grape (Shasta) | 6 fl. oz. | 30 |
| Grapefruit (Shasta) | 6 fl. oz. | 25 |
| Lemon-lime (No-Cal) | 6 fl. oz. | 29 |
| *Mr. PiBB* | 6 fl. oz. | 19 |
| Orange: | | |
| (Canada Dry; No-Cal) | 6 fl. oz. | 19 |
| (Shasta) | 6 fl. oz. | 26 |
| Quinine or tonic (No-Cal) | 6 fl. oz. | 15 |
| *RC 100* (Royal Crown) | | |
| caffeine free | 6 fl. oz. | 19 |
| Root beer: | | |
| *Barrelhead* (Canada Dry) | 6 fl. oz. | 19 |
| (Dad's) diet, | | |
| 100% NutraSweet | 6 fl. oz. | 14 |
| (Shasta) | 6 fl. oz. | 27 |
| *Seven-Up* | 6 fl. oz. | 19 |
| *Slice* | 6 fl. oz. | 2 |
| *Sprite* | 6 fl. oz. | Tr. |
| *Tab,* regular or caffeine free | 6 fl. oz. | 15 |
| **SOLE,** frozen: | | |
| (Mrs.Paul's) fillets, bread & fried, | | |
| light & natural | 1 fillet | 700 |
| (Van de Kamp's) batter dipped, | | |
| french fried | 1 piece | 289 |
| (Weight Watchers) in lemon sauce | 9⅛-oz. meal | 835 |
| **SOUFFLE, FROZEN** (Stouffer's): | | |
| Cheese | 6-oz. serving | 1260 |
| Corn | 4-oz. serving | 510 |

| Food and Description | Measure or Quantity | Sodium (mgs.) |
|---|---|---|
| **SOUP:** | | |
| Canned, regular pack: | | |
| *Asparagus (Campbell), condensed, cream of | 8-oz. serving | 900 |
| Bean (Campbell): | | |
| *Chunky*, with ham, old fashioned | 11-oz. can | 1180 |
| *Condensed, with bacon | 8-oz. serving | 875 |
| Bean, black: | | |
| *(Campbell) condensed | 8-oz. serving | 995 |
| (Crosse & Blackwell) | 6½-oz. serving | 757 |
| Beef: | | |
| (Campbell): | | |
| *Chunky:* | | |
| Regular | 10¾-oz. can | 1190 |
| Stroganoff | 10¾-oz. can | 1315 |
| *Condensed: | | |
| Regular | 8-oz. serving | 855 |
| Broth | 8-oz. serving | 875 |
| Consomme | 8-oz. serving | 785 |
| Noodle, regular | 8-oz. serving | 875 |
| (Swanson) | 7½-oz. can | 840 |
| Celery: | | |
| *(Campbell) condensed, cream of | 8-oz. serving | 875 |
| *(Rokeach): | | |
| Prepared with milk | 10-oz. serving | 1020 |
| Prepared with water | 10-oz. serving | 950 |
| *Cheddar cheese (Campbell) | 8-oz. serving | 885 |
| Chicken: | | |
| (Campbell): | | |
| *Chunky:* | | |
| Old fashioned | 10¾-oz. can | 1365 |
| & rice | 19-oz. can | 2120 |
| Vegetable | 19-oz. can | 2230 |
| *Condensed: | | |
| Alphabet | 8-oz. serving | 870 |
| Broth: | | |
| Plain | 8-oz. serving | 810 |
| & rice | 8-oz. serving | 880 |
| Cream of | 8-oz. serving | 860 |
| Mushroom, creamy | 8-oz. serving | 940 |
| *NoodleOs* | 8-oz. serving | 860 |
| & rice | 8-oz. serving | 870 |
| Vegetable | 8-oz. serving | 880 |
| *Semi-condensed, *Soup For One*, vegetable, full flavored | 11-oz. serving | 1500 |

118

| Food and Description | Measure or Quantity | Sodium (mgs.) |
|---|---|---|
| (Swanson) broth | 7¼-oz. can | 910 |
| Chili beef (Campbell) *Chunky* | 11-oz. can | 1155 |
| Chowder: | | |
| Clam: | | |
| Manhattan style: | | |
| (Campbell): | | |
| *Chunky* | 19-oz. can | 2210 |
| *Condensed | 8-oz. serving | 860 |
| (Crosse & Blackwell) | 6½-oz. serving | 803 |
| New England style: | | |
| *(Campbell): | | |
| Condensed: | | |
| Made with milk | 8-oz. serving | 940 |
| Made with water | 8-oz. serving | 885 |
| Semi-condensed, | | |
| *Soup For One:* | | |
| Made with milk | 11-oz. serving | 1420 |
| Made with water | 11-oz. serving | 1365 |
| (Crosse & Blackwell) | 6½-oz. serving | 637 |
| Consomme madrilene | | |
| (Crosse & Blackwell) | 6½-oz. serving | 609 |
| Crab (Cross & Blackwell) | 6½-oz. serving | 933 |
| Gazpacho (Crosse & Blackwell) | 6½-oz. serving | 600 |
| Ham'n butter bean (Campbell) | | |
| *Chunky* | 10¾-oz. can | 1190 |
| Lentil (Crosse & Blackwell) | | |
| with ham | 6½-oz. serving | 979 |
| *Meatball alphabet (Campbell) | | |
| condensed | 8-oz. serving | 970 |
| Minestrone: | | |
| (Campbell): | | |
| *Chunky* | 19-oz. can | 1990 |
| *Condensed | 8-oz. serving | 930 |
| (Crosse & Blackwell) | 6½-oz. serving | 720 |
| Mushroom: | | |
| *(Campbell) condensed: | | |
| Cream of | 8-oz. serving | 825 |
| Golden | 8-oz. serving | 910 |
| (Crosse & Blackwell) cream of, | | |
| bisque | 6½-oz. serving | 923 |
| *(Rokeach) cream of | | |
| Prepared with milk | 10-oz. serving | 1170 |
| Prepared with water | 10-oz. serving | 1050 |
| *Noodle (Campbell) & | | |
| ground beef | 8-oz. serving | 845 |
| *Onion (Campbell): | | |
| Regular | 8-oz. serving | 960 |

| Food and Description | Measure or Quantity | Sodium (mgs.) |
|---|---|---|
| Cream of: | | |
| Made with water | 8-oz. serving | 835 |
| Made with water & milk | 8-oz. serving | 865 |
| *Oyster stew (Campbell): | | |
| Made with milk | 8-oz. serving | 905 |
| Made with water | 8-oz. serving | 845 |
| *Pea, green (Campbell) | 8-oz. serving | 855 |
| Pea, split (Campbell): | | |
| _Chunky_, with ham | 19-oz. can | 2000 |
| *Condensed, with ham & bacon | 8-oz. serving | 810 |
| *Pepper pot (Campbell) | 8-oz. serving | 960 |
| *Potato (Campbell) cream of: | | |
| Made with water | 8-oz. serving | 960 |
| Made with water & milk | 8-oz. serving | 960 |
| Shrimp: | | |
| *(Campbell) condensed, cream of: | | |
| Made with milk | 8-oz. serving | 965 |
| Made with water | 8-oz. serving | 905 |
| (Crosse & Blackwell) | 6½-oz. serving | 1459 |
| Steak & potato (Campbell) _Chunky_ | 19-oz. can | 2230 |
| Tomato: | | |
| (Campbell): | | |
| Condensed: | | |
| Regular: | | |
| Made with milk | 8-oz. serving | 800 |
| Made with water | 8-oz. serving | 750 |
| & rice, old fashioned | 8-oz. serving | 780 |
| Semi-condensed, | | |
| _Soup For One_, Royale | 11-oz. serving | 1335 |
| *(Rokeach): | | |
| Made with milk | 10-oz. serving | 1059 |
| Made with water | 10-oz. serving | 980 |
| Turkey (Campbell) _Chunky_ & vegetable | 18¾-oz. can | 2180 |
| Vegetable: | | |
| (Campbell): | | |
| _Chunky:_ | | |
| Regular | 19-oz. can | 1990 |
| Beef, old fashioned | 19-oz. can | 2180 |
| *Condensed: | | |
| Regular | 8-oz. serving | 770 |
| Beef | 8-oz. serving | 830 |
| *Semi-condensed, | | |
| _Soup For One_, old world | 11-oz. serving | 1495 |
| *(Rokeach) vegetarian | 10-oz. serving | 1055 |

| Food and Description | Measure or Quantity | Sodium (mgs.) |
|---|---|---|
| Vichyssoise (Crosse & Blackwell) | 6½-oz. serving | 702 |
| *Won ton (Campbell) | 8-oz. serving | 875 |
| Canned, dietetic pack: | | |
| Beef (Campbell) & mushroom, low sodium | 10¾-oz. can | 75 |
| Chicken: | | |
| (Campbell) low sodium: | | |
| Broth | 10½-oz. can | 100 |
| *Chunky* | 10¾-oz. can | 100 |
| *(Dia-Mel) & noodle | 8-oz. serving | 15 |
| Mushroom (Campbell) cream of, low sodium | 10½-oz. can | 60 |
| Pea, split (Campbell) low sodium | 10¾-oz. can | 25 |
| Tomato: | | |
| (Campbell) low sodium with tomato pieces | 10½-oz. can | 40 |
| (Dia-Mel) | 8-oz. serving | 15 |
| Vegetable (Campbell) *Chunky* low sodium | 10¾-oz. can | 65 |
| Frozen: | | |
| *Barley & mushroom (Mother's Own) | 8-oz. serving | 490 |
| Chowder, clam, New England style (Stouffer's) | 8-oz. serving | 510 |
| Pea, split: | | |
| *(Mother's Own) | 8-oz. serving | 575 |
| (Stouffer's) with ham | 8¼-oz. serving | 695 |
| Spinach (Stouffer's) cream of | 8-oz. serving | 885 |
| *Vegetable (Mother's Own) | 8-oz. serving | 560 |
| *Won ton (La Choy) | 7½-oz. serving | 1050 |
| *Mix (Lipton): | | |
| Regular: | | |
| Chicken: | | |
| Regular | 8 fl. oz. | 900 |
| *Cup-A-Broth* | 6 fl. oz. | 780 |
| *Cup-A-Soup:* | | |
| Regular: | | |
| Cream of | 6 fl. oz. | 840 |
| Rice | 6 fl. oz. | 750 |
| Country style, supreme | 6 fl. oz. | 870 |
| Hearty, noodle | 8 fl. oz. | 695 |
| *Lots-A-Noodles*, cream of | 7 fl. oz. | 755 |
| Mushroom: | | |
| Regular, beef | 8 fl. oz. | 995 |
| *Cup-A-Soup*, cream of | 6 fl. oz. | 830 |
| Noodle: | | |
| Regular: | | |
| With chicken broth | 8 fl. oz. | 785 |

| Food and Description | Measure or Quantity | Sodium (mgs.) |
|---|---|---|
| *Ring-O-Noodle* | 8 fl. oz. | 855 |
| *Cup-A-Soup*, beef flavor | 6 fl. oz. | 830 |
| Onion, regular, beefy | 8 fl. oz. | 640 |
| Pea, *Cup-A-Soup*, green | 6 fl. oz. | 710 |
| Tomato, *Cup-A-Soup*, regular | 6 fl. oz. | 650 |
| Vegetable: | | |
| Regular, country | 8 fl. oz. | 995 |
| *Cup-A-Soup*, spring | 6 fl. oz. | 865 |
| Dietetic, *Cup-A-Soup-Trim*: | | |
| Beef | 6 fl. oz. | 695 |
| Chicken | 6 fl. oz. | 560 |
| Herb vegetable | 6 fl. oz. | 560 |
| **SOUP GREENS** (Durkee) | 2⅓-oz. jar | 408 |
| **SOYBEAN CURD OR TOFU** | 2¾" × 1½" × 1"cake | 8 |
| **SOYBEAN OR NUT:** | | |
| Dry roasted (*Soy Ahoy; Soy Town*) | 1 oz. | 6 |
| Oil roasted (*Soy Ahoy; Soy Town*) | | |
| plain, barbecue or garlic | 1 oz. | 6 |
| **SPAGHETTI:** | | |
| Cooked: | | |
| 8-10 minutes, "Al Dente" | 1 cup | 1 |
| 14-20 minutes, tender | 1 cup | 1 |
| Canned: | | |
| (Franco-American): | | |
| With meatballs in tomato sauce, | | |
| *SpaghettiOs* | 7⅜-oz. can | 1035 |
| In meat sauce | 7½-oz. can | 1110 |
| With sliced franks in | | |
| tomato sauce, *SpaghettiOs* | 7⅜-oz. can | 1070 |
| In tomato sauce with cheese | 7⅜-oz. can | 940 |
| (Libby's) & meatballs in | | |
| tomato sauce | 7½-oz. serving | 1359 |
| Dietetic (Dia-Mel) & meatballs | 8-oz. serving | 55 |
| Frozen: | | |
| (Banquet): entree | 8-oz. pkg. | 1242 |
| (Green Giant) & meatballs in | | |
| tomato sauce | 10-oz. entree | 989 |
| (Morton) casserole, & meat | 8-oz. casserole | 760 |
| (Stouffer's) *Lean Cuisine* | 11½-oz. pkg. | 1455 |
| **SPAGHETTI SAUCE, CANNED:** | | |
| Regular pack: | | |
| Gardenstyle (Ragú) Chunky | 3.9 oz. | 400 |
| Marinara (Prince) | 4-oz. serving | 590 |
| Meat or meat flavored: | | |
| (Prego) | 4-oz. serving | 688 |
| (Prince) | ½ cup | 626 |
| (Ragú) regular | 4 oz. | 740 |

| Food and Description | Measure or Quantity | Sodium (mgs.) |
|---|---|---|
| Meatless or plain: | | |
| (Prego) | 4-oz. serving | 676 |
| (Prince) | ½ cup | 732 |
| Mushroom: | | |
| (Prego) | 4-oz. serving | 648 |
| (Prince) | 4-oz. serving | 580 |
| Dietetic pack (Prego) | 4 oz. | 23 |
| *SPAGHETTI SAUCE MIX: | | |
| (Durkee) | ½ cup | 747 |
| (French's) with mushrooms | ⅝ cup | 900 |
| SPAM, luncheon meat (Hormel): | | |
| Regular | ¼ of 7-oz. can | 756 |
| With cheese chunks | 1-oz. serving | 405 |
| Deviled | 1 T. | 125 |
| Smoke flavored | 1-oz. serving | 387 |
| SPECIAL K, cereal (Kellogg's) | 1 cup | 220 |
| SPINACH: | | |
| Fresh, whole leaves | ½ cup | 11 |
| Boiled, without salt, drained | ½ cup | 39 |
| Canned, regular pack (Del Monte) | | |
| solids & liq. | ½ cup | 355 |
| Canned, dietetic (Larsen) | | |
| Fresh-Lite | ½ cup | 18 |
| Frozen: | | |
| (Birds Eye): | | |
| Chopped | ⅓ pkg. | 82 |
| Creamed | ⅓ pkg. | 277 |
| With water chestnuts & | | |
| seasonings | ⅓ pkg. | 239 |
| (Green Giant): | | |
| Creamed | ½ cup | 395 |
| Cut, in butter sauce | ½ cup | 465 |
| Harvest Fresh | ½ cup | 465 |
| (McKenzie) chopped | ⅓ pkg. | 70 |
| (Stouffer's) souffle | 4-oz. serving | 600 |
| SQUASH, SUMMER: | | |
| Yellow, boiled slices | ½ cup | Tr. |
| Zucchini, boiled slices | ½ cup | Tr. |
| Canned (Del Monte) zucchini, | | |
| in tomato sauce | ½ cup | 485 |
| Frozen: | | |
| (Birds Eye) zucchini | ⅓ pkg. | 3 |
| (McKenzie) Crookneck | ⅓ pkg. | 1 |
| (Mrs. Paul's) zucchini parmesan | ⅓ pkg. | 2 |
| SQUASH, WINTER: | | |
| Acorn, baked | ½ cup | 1 |
| Hubbard, baked, mashed | ½ cup | 1 |

| Food and Description | Measure or Quantity | Sodium (mgs.) |
|---|---|---|
| Frozen: | | |
| (Birds Eye) | ⅓ pkg. | 2 |
| (Southland) butternut | 4-oz. serving | 2 |
| **STEAK & GREEN PEPPERS,** | | |
| frozen: | | |
| (Green Giant) | 9-oz. entree | 1170 |
| (Swanson) | 8½-oz. entree | 1111 |
| **STOCK BASE** (French's) beef | | |
| or chicken | 1 tsp. | 470 |
| **STRAWBERRY:** | | |
| Fresh, capped | ½ cup | Tr. |
| Frozen (Birds Eye): | | |
| Halves | ⅓ pkg. | 1 |
| Whole | ¼ pkg. | Tr. |
| Whole, quick thaw | ½ pkg. | 6 |
| **STRAWBERRY DRINK** (Hi-C): | | |
| Canned | 6 fl. oz. | Tr. |
| *Mix | 6 fl. oz. | 43 |
| *STRAWBERRY KRISPIES,* cereal | | |
| (Kellogg's) | ¾ cup | 200 |
| **STRAWBERRY NECTAR,** canned | | |
| (Libby's) | 6 fl. oz. | 5 |
| **STRAWBERRY PRESERVE** | | |
| **OR JAM:** | | |
| Sweetened (Smucker's) | 1 T. | 2 |
| Dietetic or low calorie: | | |
| (Dia-Mel) | 1 T. | <3 |
| (Diet Delight) | 1 T. | 30 |
| (Estee) | 1 T. | Tr. |
| (Featherweight) artificially | | |
| sweetened | 1 T. | 40-50 |
| (Louis Sherry) | 1 T. | <3 |
| *STRAWBERRY SHORTCAKE,* | | |
| cereal (General Mills) | 1 cup | 190 |
| **STUFFING MIX:** | | |
| *Beef, Stove Top | ½ cup | 582 |
| *Chicken, *Stove Top*: | | |
| Regular | ½ cup | 650 |
| Reduced salt | ½ cup | 559 |
| Cornbread (Pepperidge Farm) | ⅛ pkg. | 530 |
| Cube or herb seasoned | | |
| (Pepperidge Farm) | 1 oz. | 510 |
| *Pork, *Stove Top* | ½ cup | 621 |
| *San Francisco Style, *Stove Top* | ½ cup | 638 |
| White bread (Mrs. Cubbison's) | 1 oz. | 480 |
| **STURGEON,** steamed | 4-oz. serving | 122 |

| Food and Description | Measure or Quantity | Sodium (mgs.) |
|---|---|---|
| **SUCCOTASH:** | | |
| Canned: | | |
| (Comstock) cream style | ½ cup | 350 |
| (Libby's) cream style | ½ cup | 317 |
| (Stokely-Van Camp) | ½ cup | 275 |
| Frozen (Birds Eye) | ⅓ pkg. | 33 |
| **SUGAR:** | | |
| Brown | 1 T. (.5 oz.) | 4 |
| Confectioners' | 1 T. | Tr. |
| Granulated | 1 T. (.4 oz.) | Tr. |
| Maple | 1¾" × 1¼" × ½" piece | 4 |
| *SUGAR CORN POPS*, cereal | | |
| (Kellogg's) | 1 cup | 95 |
| *SUGAR CRISP*, cereal (Post) | ⅞ cup | 25 |
| *SUGAR PUFFS*, cereal | | |
| (Malt-O-Meal) | ⅞ cup | 26 |
| *SUGAR SMACKS*, cereal (Kellogg's) | ¾ cup | 70 |
| **SUGAR SUBSTITUTE:** | | |
| (Estee) fructose | 1 tsp. | 0 |
| (Featherweight) | 3 drops | 5 |
| *Sprinkle Sweet* (Pillsbury) | 1 tsp. | 1 |
| *Sweet'n-it* (Dia-Mel) liquid | 5 drops | 1 |
| ***SUKIYAKI DINNER,** frozen* | | |
| (La Choy) | ¾ cup | 910 |
| **SUNFLOWER SEED** (Fisher): | | |
| In hull, roasted, salted | 1 oz. | 58 |
| Hulled, dry roasted, salted | 1 oz. | 108 |
| Hulled, oil roasted, salted | 1 oz. | 108 |
| *SUZY Q* (Hostess): | | |
| Banana | 1 piece | 195 |
| Chocolate | 1 piece | 300 |
| **SWEET POTATO:** | | |
| Baked, peeled | 5" × 1" potato | 13 |
| Canned, heavy syrup | 4-oz. serving | 54 |
| Frozen: | | |
| (Mrs. Paul's) candied, with apple | 4-oz. serving | 150 |
| (Stouffer's) & apples | 5-oz. serving | 225 |
| **SWEET & SOUR PORK,** frozen: | | |
| (La Choy) | 12-oz. entree | 2200 |
| (Van de Kamp's) | 11-oz. serving | 590 |
| **SWISS STEAK,** frozen (Swanson) | 10-oz. dinner | 830 |
| **SYRUP** (See also TOPPING): | | |
| Regular: | | |
| Apricot (Smucker's) | 1 T. | 5 |
| Blackberry (Smucker's) | 1 T. | 2 |
| Chocolate or chocolate-flavored: | | |
| *Bosco* | 1 T. | 25 |

| Food and Description | Measure or Quantity | Sodium (mgs.) |
|---|---|---|
| (Hershey's) | 1 T. | 8 |
| (Nestlé) *Quik* | 1 oz. | 35 |
| Corn, *Karo,* dark or light | 1 T. | 37 |
| Maple, *Karo,* imitation | 1 T. | 32 |
| Pancake or waffle: | | |
| (Aunt Jemima) | 1 T. | 15 |
| *Golden Griddle* | 1 T. | 20 |
| *Karo* | 1 T. | 32 |
| *Log Cabin,* regular or buttered | 1 T. | 6 |
| *Mrs. Butterworth's* | 1 T. | 24 |
| Strawberry (Smucker's) | 1 T. | 2 |
| Dietetic or low calorie: | | |
| Blueberry (Featherweight) | 1 T. | <25 |
| Chocolate or chocolate-flavored | | |
| (Diet Delight) | 1 T. | 10 |
| Pancake or waffle: | | |
| (Aunt Jemima) | 1 T. | 29 |
| (Dia-Mel) | 1 T. | 10 |
| (Diet Delight) | 1 T. | 30 |
| (Featherweight) | 1 T. | <25 |

# T

| Food and Description | Measure or Quantity | Sodium (mgs.) |
|---|---|---|
| **TACO:** | | |
| *(Ortega) | 1 taco | 420 |
| *Mix (Durkee) | ½ cup | 557 |
| Shell (Ortega) | 1 shell | 55 |
| **TAMALE:** | | |
| Canned (Hormel) beef, *Short Orders* | 7½-oz. can | 1140 |
| Frozen (Hormel) beef | 1 tamale | 555 |
| ***TANG:*** | | |
| Grape | 6 fl. oz. | 5 |
| Orange | 6 fl. oz. | 1 |
| **TANGERINE OR MANDARIN ORANGE:** | | |
| Fresh (Sunkist) | 1 large tangerine | 2 |
| Canned, solids & liq.: | | |
| Regular pack (Del Monte) | 5½-oz. serving | <10 |
| Dietetic pack: | | |
| (Diet Delight) juice pack | ½ cup | 5 |
| (Featherweight) water pack | ½ cup | <10 |
| **TANGERINE DRINK,** canned (Hi-C) | 6 fl. oz. | <1 |
| ***TANGERINE JUICE,*** frozen (Minute Maid) | 6 fl. oz. | 2 |
| **TAPIOCA,** dry, *Minute,* quick cooking | 1 T. | Tr. |
| **TAQUITO,** frozen (Van de Kamp's) beef | 8-oz. serving | 771 |
| **TARRAGON** (French's) | 1 tsp. | 1 |
| ***TASTEEOS,*** cereal (Ralston Purina) | 1¼ cups | 210 |
| ***TEA:*** | | |
| Bag | 1 bag | 0 |
| Instant (Lipton) | 8 fl. oz. | 0 |
| ***TEA MIX, ICED:*** | | |
| Regular, *Country Time* | 1 cup | Tr. |
| Dietetic, *Crystal Light* | 1 cup | Tr. |

| Food and Description | Measure or Quantity | Sodium (mgs.) |
|---|---|---|
| **TEQUILA SUNRISE COCKTAIL** | | |
| (Mr. Boston) 12 ½% alcohol | 3 fl. oz. | 130 |
| **TERIYAKI**, frozen (Stouffer's) | 10-oz. serving | 1450 |
| **\*TEXTURED VEGETABLE** | | |
| **PROTEIN**, *Morningstar Farms:* | | |
| Breakfast link | 1 link | 225 |
| Breakfast patties | 1 patty | 470 |
| Breakfast strips | 1 strip | 124 |
| *Grillers* | 1 patty | 334 |
| **THURINGER:** | | |
| (Eckrich) sliced | 1-oz. slice | 380 |
| (Hormel): | | |
| Packaged, sliced | 1 slice | 380 |
| *Old Smokehouse* | 1-oz. serving | 328 |
| (Oscar Mayer) | .8-oz. slice | 317 |
| *TIGER TAIL* (Hostess) | 2¼-oz. piece | 240 |
| **TOASTER CAKE OR PASTRY:** | | |
| *Pop-Tarts* (Kellogg's): | | |
| Regular: | | |
| Blueberry | 1 pastry | 220 |
| Brown sugar cinnamon | 1 pastry | 215 |
| Cherry | 1 pastry | 230 |
| Frosted: | | |
| Blueberry | 1 pastry | 220 |
| Brown sugar cinnamon | 1 pastry | 205 |
| Cherry | 1 pastry | 230 |
| Chocolate-vanilla creme | 1 pastry | 220 |
| Strawberry | 1 pastry | 215 |
| Toaster Strudel (Pillsbury) | | |
| blueberry or strawberry | 1 pastry | 205 |
| *Toast-R-Cake* (Thomas'): | | |
| Blueberry | 1 piece | 283 |
| Bran | 1 piece | 316 |
| Corn | 1 piece | 332 |
| *TOASTIES*, cereal (Post) | 1¼ cups | 298 |
| *TOASTY O's*, cereal (Malt-O-Meal) | 1¼ cup | 281 |
| **TOMATO:** | | |
| Regular, whole, ripe | 1 med. tomato | 4 |
| Canned, regular pack, solids & liq.: | | |
| (Contadina) sliced, baby | ½ cup | 465 |
| (Del Monte) stewed | 4 oz. | 355 |
| (Stokely-Van Camp) stewed | ½ cup | 190 |
| Canned, dietetic pack, solids & liq.: | | |
| (Del Monte) No Salt Added | ½ cup | 45 |
| (Diet Delight) | ½ cup | 15 |
| (Featherweight) | ½ cup | <10 |

| Food and Description | Measure or Quantity | Sodium (mgs.) |
|---|---|---|
| **TOMATO JUICE,** canned: | | |
| Regular pack: | | |
| (Campbell) | 6-fl.-oz. can | 625 |
| (Del Monte) | 6-fl.-oz. can | 478 |
| (Libby's) | 6-fl.-oz. can | 455 |
| Dietetic pack (Diet Delight; | | |
| Featherweight) | 6 fl. oz. | 29 |
| **TOMATO JUICE COCKTAIL,** | | |
| canned: | | |
| (Ocean Spray) *Firehouse Jubilee* | 6 fl. oz. | 599 |
| *Snap-E-Tom* | 6 fl. oz. | 980 |
| **TOMATO PASTE,** canned: | | |
| Regular pack: | | |
| (Contadina) Italian | 6-oz. serving | 2130 |
| (Del Monte) | 6-oz. can | 110 |
| Dietetic (Del Monte) | | |
| No Salt Added | 6-oz. can | 110 |
| **TOMATO & PEPPER, HOT CHILI** | | |
| (Ortega) Jalapeno | 1-oz. serving | 119 |
| **TOMATO, PICKLED** (Claussen) | | |
| green | 1 piece | 326 |
| **TOMATO PUREE,** canned: | | |
| Regular (Contadina) heavy | 1 cup | 180 |
| Dietetic (Featherweight) | 1 cup | <20 |
| **TOMATO SAUCE,** canned: | | |
| (Contadina) regular | 1 cup | 510 |
| (Del Monte): | | |
| Regular | ½ cup | 665 |
| Hot | ½ cup | 679 |
| With tomato bits | ½ cup | 497 |
| No Salt Added | ½ cup | 25 |
| (Hunt's) with cheese | 4-oz. serving | 836 |
| **TOM COLLINS,** (Mr. Boston) | | |
| 12½% alcohol | 3 fl. oz. | 39 |
| **TONGUE:** | | |
| Beef, braised | 4-oz. serving | 69 |
| Canned (Hormel) cured | 3 oz. | 966 |
| **TOPPING:** | | |
| Regular: | | |
| Butterscotch (Smucker's) | 1 T. | 46 |
| Caramel (Smucker's) | 1 T. | 55 |
| Chocolate fudge (Hershey's) | 1 T. | 16 |
| Pineapple (Smucker's) | 1 T. | 25 |
| Dietetic, chocolate (Diet Delight) | 1 T. | 9 |
| **TOPPING, WHIPPED:** | | |
| Regular: | | |
| *Cool Whip* (Birds Eye) dairy | 1 T. | 2 |

| Food and Description | Measure or Quantity | Sodium (mgs.) |
|---|---|---|
| *Dover Farms* | 1 T. | 3 |
| *Lucky Whip,* aerosol | 1 T. | 4 |
| *Whip Topping* (Rich's) | ¼ oz. | 5 |
| Dietetic (Featherweight) | 1 T. | Tr. |
| *Mix: | | |
| Regular, *Dream Whip* | 1 T. | 4 |
| Dietetic (D-Zerta) | 1 T. | 4 |
| **TORTILLA,** (Old El Paso) | 1 oz. | 193 |
| **TOSTADA,** frozen (Van de Kamp's) | 8½-oz. serving | 720 |
| **TOSTADA SHELL** (Ortega) | 1 shell | 72 |
| *TOTAL*, cereal: | | |
| Regular | 1 cup | 375 |
| Corn | 1 cup | 310 |
| **TRIPE,** canned (Libby's) | 6-oz. serving | 147 |
| *TRIX,* cereal (General Mills) | 1 cup | 170 |
| **TUNA:** | | |
| Canned in oil (Bumble Bee): | | |
| Chunk, light, drained | ½ cup | 327 |
| Solids, white, drained | ½ cup | 414 |
| Canned in water: | | |
| (Bumble Bee): | | |
| Chunk, light, drained | ½ cup | 311 |
| Solid, white, drained | ½ cup | 333 |
| (Featherweight) light, chunk | 6½-oz. can | 93 |
| *TUNA HELPER* (General Mills): | | |
| Country dumplings | ⅕ pkg. | 1020 |
| Creamy noodle | ⅕ pkg. | 880 |
| **TUNA NOODLE CASSEROLE,** frozen (Stouffer's) | 5¾-oz. serving | 670 |
| **TUNA PIE,** frozen: | | |
| (Banquet) | 8-oz. pie | 1305 |
| (Morton) | 8-oz. pie | 1120 |
| **TUNA SALAD,** canned (Carnation) | ¼ of 7½-oz. can | 270 |
| **TURKEY:** | | |
| Canned: | | |
| (Hormel) chunk | 6¾-oz. serving | 1278 |
| (Swanson) chunk | 2½-oz. serving | 380 |
| (Hormel) breast | .8-oz. slice | 242 |
| (Oscar Mayer) breast | ¾-oz. slice | 295 |
| Roasted: | | |
| Dark meat | 2½" × 1⅝" × ¼" slice | 21 |
| Light meat | 4" × 2" × ¼" slice | 35 |
| **TURKEY DINNER OR ENTREE, FROZEN:** | | |
| (Banquet): | | |
| American Favorites | 11-oz. dinner | 1416 |
| Extra Helping | 19-oz. dinner | 2165 |

| Food and Description | Measure or Quantity | Sodium (mgs.) |
|---|---|---|
| (Morton) | 5-oz. entree | 640 |
| (Green Giant): | 9-oz. entree | 404 |
| (Swanson): | | |
|   Regular | 8¾-oz. entree | 1070 |
|   *Hungry Man* | 18½-oz. dinner | 2110 |
| (Weight Watchers) sliced, | | |
|   3-compartment | 15¼-oz. meal | 1775 |
| **TURKEY, PIE,** frozen: | | |
| (Banquet): | | |
|   Regular | 8-oz. pie | 1111 |
|   Supreme | 8-oz. pie | 1370 |
| (Morton) | 8-oz. pie | 1115 |
| (Stouffer's) | 10-oz. pie | 1735 |
| (Swanson) regular | 8-oz. pie | 890 |
| **TURKEY TETRAZINI,** frozen: | | |
| (Stouffer's) | 6-oz. serving | 620 |
| (Weight Watchers) | 10-oz. serving | 872 |
| **TURMERIC** (French's) | 1 tsp. | Tr. |
| **TURNIP GREENS:** | | |
| Canned (Sunshine) chopped, | | |
|   solids & liq. | ½ cup | 252 |
| Frozen (Birds Eye) chopped | ⅓ pkg. | 11 |
| **TURNOVER:** | | |
| Frozen (Pepperidge Farm): | | |
|   Apple | 1 turnover | 215 |
|   Blueberry | 1 turnover | 235 |
|   Cherry | 1 turnover | 285 |
|   Peach | 1 turnover | 266 |
| Refrigerated (Pillsbury): | | |
|   Apple or blueberry | 1 turnover | 305 |
|   Cherry | 1 turnover | 310 |
| ***TWINKIE*** (Hostess) | 1 piece | 150 |

# U

| Food and Description | Measure or Quantity | Sodium (mgs.) |
|---|---|---|
| **UFO'S,** canned (Franco-American): | | |
| Regular | 7½-oz. can | 780 |
| With meteors | 7½-oz. can | 790 |

# V

| Food and Description | Measure or Quantity | Sodium (mgs.) |
|---|---|---|
| **VEAL,** broiled, medium cooked, loin chop, rib, roasted or steak or cutlet, lean & fat | 4 oz. | 91 |
| **VEAL DINNER, FROZEN:** | | |
| (Banquet) parmigiana: | | |
| Casserole | 1-lb. pkg. | 4210 |
| Dinner, Extra Helping | 20-oz. dinner | 2123 |
| (Morton) parmigiana | 20-oz. dinner | 2430 |
| (Swanson) parmigiana: | | |
| Regular | 12¾-oz. dinner | 1280 |
| *Hungry Man* | 20½-oz. dinner | 2075 |
| (Weight Watchers) parmigiana, 2-compartment | 9-oz. meal | 1003 |
| **VEGETABLE BOUILLON** (Herb-Ox): | | |
| Cube | 1 cube | 920 |
| Packet | 1 packet | 880 |
| **VEGETABLE FLAKES** (French's) | 1 T. | 20 |
| **VEGETABLE JUICE COCKTAIL:** | | |
| Regular, *V-8* | 6 fl. oz. | 625 |
| Dietetic: | | |
| (S&W) *Nutradiet,* low sodium | 6 fl. oz. | 25 |
| *V-8,* low sodium | 6 fl. oz. | 50 |
| **VEGETABLES, MIXED:** | | |
| Canned, regular pack: | | |
| (Del Monte) solids & liq. | ½ cup | 355 |
| (La Choy), drained: | | |
| Chinese | ⅓ of 13-oz. pkg. | 350 |
| Chop Suey | ½ cup | 315 |
| (Libby's) solids & liq. | ½ cup | 345 |
| Canned, dietetic pack: | | |
| (Featherweight) | ½ cup | 25 |
| (Larsen) *Fresh-Lite* | ½ cup | 25 |
| Frozen: | | |
| (Birds Eye): | | |
| Regular: | | |

| Food and Description | Measure or Quantity | Sodium (mgs.) |
|---|---|---|
| Broccoli, cauliflower & carrots in cheese sauce | ⅓ pkg. | 263 |
| Carrots, peas & onions, deluxe | ⅓ pkg. | 62 |
| Mixed, with onion sauce | ½ pkg. | 357 |
| Pea & pearl onion | ⅓ pkg. | 311 |
| *Blue Ribbon:* | | |
| Broccoli, carrots & pasta in lightly seasoned sauce | ⅓ pkg. | 274 |
| Corn, green beans & pasta in lightly seasoned sauce | ⅓ pkg. | 282 |
| *Farm Fresh:* | | |
| Broccoli, cauliflower & carrot strips | 3.2 oz. | 30 |
| Brussels sprouts, cauliflower & carrots | 3.2 oz. | 20 |
| *International Style:* | | |
| Chinese style | ⅓ pkg. | 360 |
| Mexican style | ⅓ pkg. | 466 |
| *Stir Fry:* | | |
| Chinese style | ⅓ pkg. | 475 |
| Japanese style | ⅓ pkg. | 566 |
| (Green Giant): | | |
| Regular: | | |
| Broccoli, cauliflower & carrots in cheese sauce | ½ cup | 465 |
| Mixed | ½ cup | 35 |
| *Harvest Fresh* | ½ cup | 220 |
| *Harvest Get Togethers:* | | |
| Broccoli-cauliflower medley | ½ cup | 470 |
| Broccoli fanfare | ½ cup | 455 |
| Japanese style | ½ cup | 155 |
| (La Choy), Chinese | 3.3-oz. serving | 540 |
| (Le Sueur) peas, onions & carrots in butter sauce | ⅓ pkg. | 100 |
| **VEGETABLES IN PASTRY, FROZEN** (Pepperidge Farm): | | |
| Asparagus with mornay sauce or broccoli with cheese | 3¾ oz. | 245 |
| Cauliflower & cheese sauce | 3¾ oz. | 465 |
| Spinach almondine | 3¾ oz. | 325 |
| Zucchini provencal | 3¾ oz. | 290 |
| **VEGETABLE STEW,** canned *Dinty Moore* (Hormel) | 8-oz. serving | 1047 |
| **"VEGETARIAN FOODS":** | | |
| Canned or dry: | | |
| Chicken, fried (Loma Linda) with gravy | 1½-oz. piece | 340 |

| Food and Description | Measure or Quantity | Sodium (mgs.) |
|---|---|---|
| Chili (Worthington) | ½ cup | 626 |
| Choplet (Worthington) | 1 choplet | 220 |
| Dinner cuts (Loma Linda) drained | 1 piece (2.1 oz.) | 330 |
| Franks, big (Loma Linda) | 1.8-oz. frank | 220 |
| Franks, sizzle (Loma Linda) | 1.2-oz. frank | 170 |
| FriChik (Worthington) | 1 piece | 406 |
| Granburger (Worthington) | 1 oz. | 622 |
| Little links (Loma Linda) drained | .8-oz. link | 105 |
| Non-meatballs (Worthington) | 1 meatball | 36 |
| Nuteena (Loma Linda) | ½" slice | 120 |
| Proteena (Loma Linda) | ½" slice | 460 |
| Sandwich spread (Loma Linda) | 1 T. | 100 |
| Soyameat (Worthington): | | |
|   Beef, sliced | 1 slice | 183 |
|   Chicken, diced | 1 oz. | 177 |
|   Salisbury steak | 1 slice | 403 |
| Soyamel, any kind (Worthington) | 1 oz. | 163 |
| Stew pack (Loma Linda) drained | 2 oz. | 220 |
| Super links (Worthington) | 1 link | 449 |
| Swiss steak with gravy (Loma Linda) | 1 steak | 350 |
| Tender bits (Loma Linda) drained | 1 piece | 85 |
| Vegelona (Loma Linda) | ½" slice | 210 |
| Vega-links (Worthington) | 1 link | 169 |
| Worthington 209 | 1 slice | 229 |
| Frozen: | | |
|   Beef-like slices (Worthington) | 1 slice | 140 |
|   Beef pie (Worthington) | 1 pie | 1109 |
|   Bologna (Loma Linda) | 1 oz. | 245 |
|   Chicken, fried (Loma Linda) | 2-oz. serving | 510 |
|   Chicken pie (Worthington) | 1 pie | 930 |
|   Chic-Ketts (Worthington) | 1 oz. | 185 |
|   Corned beef, loaf or sliced (Worthington) | ½ oz. | 155 |
|   FriPats (Worthington) | 1 pat | 379 |
|   Meatballs (Loma Linda) | 1 piece | 53 |
|   Prosage (Worthington) | 1 link | 140 |
|   Smoked beef, sliced (Worthington) | ¼ oz. | 99 |
| VERMOUTH sweet (Great Western) | 3 fl. oz. | 20 |
| VICHY WATER (Schweppes) | 6 fl. oz. | 80 |
| VINEGAR | 1 T. | Tr. |

# W

| Food and Description | Measure or Quantity | Sodium (mgs.) |
|---|---|---|
| **WAFFELOS,** cereal (Ralston Purina) | 1 cup | 116 |
| **WAFFLE,** frozen: | | |
| (Aunt Jemima) jumbo | 1 waffle | 261 |
| (Eggo): | | |
| Blueberry | 1 waffle | 260 |
| Strawberry | 1 waffle | 265 |
| Home style | 1 waffle | 265 |
| **WALNUT,** English or Persian | 1 cup | 2 |
| **WATER CHESTNUT,** canned | | |
| (La Choy) drained | ¼ of 8-oz. can | <15 |
| **WATERCRESS,** trimmed | ½ cup | 8 |
| **WATERMELON:** | | |
| Wedge | 4″ × 8″ wedge | 4 |
| Diced | ½ cup | 1 |
| **WELSH RAREBIT:** | | |
| Home recipe | 1 cup | 770 |
| Frozen (Stouffer's) | 5-oz. serving | 660 |
| **WENDY'S** | | |
| Bacon, breakfast | 1 strip | 223 |
| Bacon cheeseburger on white bun | 1 burger | 860 |
| Breakfast sandwich | 1 sandwich | |
| Buns: | | |
| Wheat, multi-grain | 1 bun | 220 |
| White | 1 bun | 266 |
| Chicken sandwich on multi-grain bun | 1 sandwich | 500 |
| Chili: | | |
| Regular | 8 oz. | 1070 |
| Large | 12 oz. | 1605 |
| Condiments: | | |
| Bacon | ½ strip | 112 |
| Cheese, American | 1 slice | 260 |
| Ketchup | 1 tsp. | 65 |
| Mayonaise | 1 T. | 80 |
| Mustard | 1 tsp. | 50 |
| Onion rings | .3-oz. piece | 0 |

136

| Food and Description | Measure or Quantity | Sodium (mgs.) |
|---|---|---|
| Pickle, dill | 4 slices | 125 |
| Relish | .3-oz. serving | 70 |
| Tomato | 1 slice | 0 |
| Danish | 1 piece | 340 |
| Drinks: | | |
| Coffee | 6 fl. oz. | 0 |
| Cola: | | |
| Regular | 12 fl. oz | 15 |
| Dietetic | 12 fl. oz. | 20 |
| Fruit flavored drink | 12 fl. oz. | 10 |
| Hot chocolate | 6 fl. oz. | 145 |
| Milk: | | |
| Regular | 8 fl. oz. | 120 |
| Chocolate | 8 fl. oz. | 150 |
| Non-cola | 12 fl. oz. | 35 |
| Orange juice | 6 fl. oz. | 0 |
| Egg, scrambled | 1 order | 160 |
| Frosty dairy dessert: | | |
| Small | 12 fl. oz | 220 |
| Medium | 16 fl. oz | 293 |
| Large | 20 fl. oz | 367 |
| Hamburger: | | |
| Double, on white bun | 1 burger | 575 |
| Kids Meal | 1 burger | 265 |
| Single: | | |
| On wheat bun | 1 burger | 290 |
| On white bun | 1 burger | 410 |
| Omelet: | | |
| Ham & cheese | 1 omelet | 405 |
| Ham, cheese & mushroom | 1 omelet | 570 |
| Ham, cheese, onion & green pepper | 1 omelet | 485 |
| Mushroom, onion & green pepper | 1 omelet | 200 |
| Potato: | | |
| Baked, hot stuffed: | | |
| Plain | 1 potato | 60 |
| Bacon & cheese | 1 potato | 1180 |
| Broccoli & cheese | 1 potato | 430 |
| Cheese | 1 potato | 450 |
| Chicken à la King | 1 potato | 820 |
| Chili & cheese | 1 potato | 610 |
| Sour cream & chives | 1 potato | 230 |
| Stroganoff & sour cream | 1 potato | 910 |
| French fries | regular order | 95 |
| Home fries | 1 order | 745 |
| Salad Bar, Garden Spot: | | |
| Alfalfa sprouts | 2 Oz. | NA |
| Bacon bits | ⅛ oz. | 95 |

| Food and Description | Measure or Quantity | Sodium (mgs.) |
|---|---|---|
| Blueberries, fresh | 1 T. | 0 |
| Breadstick | 1 piece | NA |
| Broccoli | ½ cup | 10 |
| Cantaloupe | 1 piece (2 oz.) | 35 |
| Carrot | ¼ cup | 15 |
| Cauliflower | ½ cup | 5 |
| Cheese: | | |
| American, imitation | 1 oz. | NA |
| Cheddar, imitation | 1 oz. | 450 |
| Cottage | ½ cup | 425 |
| Mozzarella, imitation | 1 oz. | 320 |
| Swiss, imitation | 1 oz. | 450 |
| Chow mein noodles | ¼ cup | 80 |
| Cole slaw | ½ cup | 70 |
| Cracker, saltine | 1 piece | 37 |
| Crouton | 1 piece | 5 |
| Cucumber | ¼ cup | 0 |
| Eggs | 1 T. | 10 |
| Mushrooms | ¼ cup | 5 |
| Onions, red | 1 T. | 0 |
| Orange, fresh | 1 piece | 0 |
| Pasta salad | ½ cup | 400 |
| Peas, green | ½ cup | 90 |
| Peaches, in syrup | 1 piece | 0 |
| Peppers: | | |
| Banana or mild pepperoncini | 1 T. | NA |
| Bell | ¼ cup | 5 |
| Jalapeno | 1 T. | 4 |
| Pineapple chunks in juice | ½ cup | 0 |
| Sunflower seeds & raisins | ¼ cup | 10 |
| Tomato | 1 oz. | 0 |
| Turkey ham | ¼ cup | NA |
| Watermelon, fresh | 1 piece (1 oz.) | 0 |
| Salad dressing: | | |
| Regular: | | |
| Blue cheese | 1 T. | 85 |
| Celery seed | 1 T. | 65 |
| French, red | 1 T. | 130 |
| Italian, golden | 1 T. | 260 |
| Oil | 1 T. | 0 |
| Ranch | 1 T. | 155 |
| Thousand Island | 1 T. | 115 |
| Dietetic: | | |
| Bacon & tomato | 1 T. | 160 |
| Cucumber, creamy | 1 T. | 140 |
| Italian | 1 T. | 180 |
| Thousand Island | 1 T. | 125 |

| Food and Description | Measure or Quantity | Sodium (mgs.) |
|---|---|---|
| Wine vinegar | 1 T. | 5 |
| Salad, Side, pick-up window | 1 salad | 540 |
| Salad, taco | 1 salad | 1100 |
| Sausage | 1 patty | 410 |
| Toast: | | |
| Regular, with margarine | 1 slice | 205 |
| French | 1 slice | 425 |
| **WESTERN DINNER,** frozen: | | |
| (Banquet) | 11-oz. dinner | 1548 |
| (Morton) | 11.8-oz. dinner | 1650 |
| (Swanson): | | |
| Regular | 12¼-oz. dinner | 1040 |
| *Hungry Man* | 17½-oz. dinner | 1900 |
| *WHEATENA,* cereal | ¼ cup | <5 |
| **WHEAT FLAKES CEREAL** | | |
| (Featherweight) | 1¼ cups | 5 |
| **WHEAT GERM, RAW** (Elam's) | 1 T. | 1 |
| **WHEAT GERM CEREAL** | | |
| (Kretschmer) | ¼ cup | <5 |
| *WHEAT HEARTS,* cereal (General | | |
| Mills) | 1 oz. | <5 |
| *WHEATIES,* cereal | 1 cup | 370 |
| **WHEAT & OATMEAL CEREAL,** | | |
| hot (Elam's) | 1 oz. | 11 |
| **WHISKEY SOUR COCKTAIL** | | |
| (Mr. Boston) | 3 fl. oz. | 59 |
| **WHITEFISH, LAKE,** baked, stuffed | 4 oz. | 221 |
| Smoked | 4 oz. | 176 |
| **WILD BERRY DRINK,** canned | | |
| (Hi-C) | 6 fl. oz. | 5 |
| **WINE, COOKING** (Regina): | | |
| Burgundy or sauterne | ¼ cup | 365 |
| Sherry | ¼ cup | 370 |

# Y

| Food and Description | Measure or Quantity | Sodium (mgs.) |
|---|---|---|
| **YEAST, BAKER'S** (Fleischmann's): | | |
| Dry, active | ¼ oz. | 7 |
| Fresh & household, active | .6-oz. cake | 5 |
| **YOGURT:** | | |
| Regular: | | |
| Plain: | | |
| (Dannon) | 8-oz. container | 115 |
| (Whitney's) | 6-oz. container | 140 |
| *Yoplait* | 6-oz. container | 135 |
| Plain with honey, *Yoplait,* | | |
| *Custard Style* | 6-oz. container | 110 |
| Apple: | | |
| (Dannon) Dutch | 8-oz. container | 70-125 |
| *Melangé* | 6-oz. container | 120 |
| *Yoplait* | 6-oz. container | 120 |
| Apple-cinnamon, *Yoplait,* | | |
| *Breakfast Yogurt* | 6-oz. container | 95 |
| Apple-raisins (Whitney's) | 6-oz. container | 95 |
| Banana (Dannon) | 8-oz. container | 70-125 |
| Blueberry: | | |
| (Dannon) | 8-oz. container | 70-125 |
| *Melangé* | 6-oz. container | 120 |
| (Sweet'n Low) | 8-oz. container | 170 |
| (Whitney's) | 6-oz. container | 95 |
| *Yoplait* | 6-oz. container | 120 |
| Boysenberry: | | |
| (Dannon) | 8-oz. container | 70-125 |
| (Sweet'n Low) | 8-oz. container | 170 |
| (Whitney's) | 6-oz. container | 95 |
| Cherry: | | |
| (Dannon) | 8-oz. container | 70-125 |
| *Melangé* | 6-oz. container | 120 |
| (Sweet'n Low) | 8-oz. container | 170 |
| *Yoplait* | 6-oz. container | 120 |
| Citrus, *Yoplait, Breakfast Yogurt* | 6-oz. container | 95 |

| Food and Description | Measure or Quantity | Sodium (mgs.) |
|---|---|---|
| Coffee (Whitney's) | 6-oz. container | 125 |
| Lemon: | | |
| (Dannon) | 8-oz. container | 70-90 |
| (Sweet'n Low) | 8-oz. container | 170 |
| (Whitney's) | 6-oz. container | 125 |
| *Yoplait:* | | |
| Regular | 6-oz. container | 120 |
| *Custard Style* | 6-oz. container | 105 |
| Orange, *Yoplait* | 6-oz. container | 120 |
| Orchard, *Yoplait,* | | |
| *Breakfast Yogurt* | 6-oz. container | 95 |
| Peach: | | |
| (Dannon) | 8-oz. container | 70-125 |
| (Sweet'n Low) | 8-oz. container | 170 |
| (Whitney's) | 6-oz. container | 95 |
| Pina colada (Dannon) | 8-oz. container | 70-125 |
| Pineapple, *Melangé* | 6-oz. container | 120 |
| Raspberry: | | |
| (Dannon) red | 8-oz. container | 70-125 |
| *Melangé* | 6-oz. container | 120 |
| (Sweet'n Low) | 8-oz. container | 170 |
| (Whitney's) | 6-oz. container | 95 |
| *Yoplait:* | | |
| Regular | 6-oz. container | 120 |
| *Custard Style* | 6-oz. container | 105 |
| Strawberry: | | |
| (Dannon) | 8-oz. container | 70-125 |
| *Melangé* | 6-oz. container | 120 |
| (Sweet'n Low) | 8-oz. container | 170 |
| *Yoplait* | 6-oz. container | 120 |
| Tropical fruit (Sweet'N Low) | 8-oz. container | 170 |
| Vanilla: | | |
| (Dannon) | 8-oz. container | 70-90 |
| (Whitney's) | 6-oz. container | 125 |
| *Yoplait, Custard Style* | 6-oz. container | 110 |
| Frozen, hard (Dannon) | | |
| Danny-On-A-Stick, chocolate, raspberry, strawberry or vanilla, chocolate coated | 2½-fl.-oz. bar | 15 |

# Z

| Food and Description | Measure or Quantity | Sodium (mgs.) |
| --- | --- | --- |
| **ZITI, FROZEN** (Weight Watchers) | 11¼-oz. serving | 1349 |
| **ZWEIBACK** (Gerber; Nabisco) | 1 piece | 16 |

Now you can say "yes" to crispy spiced duck, egg rolls, shrimp lo mein, and all your other favorite Chinese dishes—while saying "no" to added salt and MSG . . .

# THE CHINESE SALT-FREE DIET COOKBOOK
## by Merle Schell

Author of
*Tasting Good: The International Salt-Free Diet Cookbook*

Without sacrificing any of the zesty tastes and textures of Chinese Cooking, these 250 low-salt, low-sugar, low-fat recipes make this popular cuisine healthier for everyone. You'll also find these helpful features:

- Taste-alike substitutes for soy sauce, black bean sauce, and many other seasonings
- Sodium, calorie, fat, and carbohydrate counts for every recipe
- Information on adapting recipes to your own needs
- A two-week diet plan based on 1200 calories and 500mg. of sodium a day
- Tables of nutritional values for ingredients used
- Complete party menus for dinners, brunches, and buffets

**"Follows in the illustrious salt-free writings of James Beard. One can enjoy Chinese cooking without salt— something few of us believed possible."**

—Frank Field, Health and Science Editor,
*CBS Morning News*

*"French cookery skillfully adapted for healthful eating . . ."*
**—Nathan Pritkin**

# *Deliciously Low*
## THE GOURMET GUIDE TO LOW-SODIUM, LOW-FAT, LOW-CHOLESTEROL, LOW-SUGAR COOKING

### *by*
### *Harriet Roth*

**Former director, Pritkin Longevity Center Cooking School**

Delight your tastebuds while protecting your health—with this unique collection of spectacular "alternative" recipes from a noted pioneer in low-risk, high-quality cooking.

- More than 300 creative and exciting recipes
- Complete nutritional information, including per-serving content of 20 essential nutrients for each dish
- Sample menus, technique lessons, and hints for garnishing, serving, and storing, and much more

"An excellent choice for the gourmet cook who decides it's time to cut down on sodium, fat, cholesterol and sugar."

**—Dr. Jean Mayer,** *Los Angeles Times*

Helpful suggestions and alternatives to sugar-laden desserts."

**—Bon Appétit**

## SIGNET Books for Your Reference Shelf

**Buy them at your local
bookstore or use coupon
on next page for ordering.**

## From the SIGNET Recipe Collection

(0451)

☐ **THE ART OF MEXICAN COOKING by Jay Aaron and Georgine Sachs Salon.** Over 300 festive and flavorful recipes, including regional specialties from all over the country. (114337—$2.95)*

☐ **EVERYDAY FRENCH COOKING by Henri-Paul Pellaprat.** A former Cordon Bleu professor has written an easy-to-use, complete French cookbook. (116801—$3.95)

☐ **THE TAPPAN CREATIVE COOKBOOK FOR MICROWAVE OVENS AND RANGES by Sylvia Schur.** Over 400 delicious recipes provided, ranging from simple breakfasts to gourmet feasts, all of which can be prepared using either a microwave or standard stove. (120396—$3.50)

☐ **THE EASY WAY TO CHINESE COOKING by Beverly Lee.** In this practical, easy-to-follow guide to authentic Chinese cooking, Beverly Lee shows how to make delicious Chinese dishes—from the simplest to the most festive and elaborate. Included is a list of Chinese stores throughout the U.S. which carry the items listed in the book. (129431—$2.95)*

☐ **ORIENTAL COOKING THE FAST WOK WAY by Jacqueline Hériteau.** Here are 150 delicious recipes made quick and easy through the art of stir-frying. This fabulous book also includes how to use a wok, the art of cutting, chopping and stir-frying ingredients—where to buy them and how to use them—and complete dinner menus. (133668—$2.95)*

☐ **CHINESE MEATLESS COOKING by Stella Lau Fessler.** Revised and updated. More than 180 recipes—a complete guide to mastering one of the world's most tempting and healthful cuisines. Illustrated by Janet Nelson. (123514—$3.50)*

*Prices slightly higher in Canada

---